INTO THE EUROPEAN MIRROR
A work by Julian Samuel

INTO THE EUROPEAN MIRROR
A work by Julian Samuel

edited by
Aruna Handa & John Kipphoff

Montréal/New York
London

Copyright © 1997 BLACK ROSE BOOKS LTD.

No part of this book may be reproduced or transmitted in any form, by any means electronic or mechanical, including photocopying and recording, or by any information storage or retrieval system — without written permission from the publisher, or, in the case of photocopying or other reprographic copying, a license from the Canadian Reprography Collective, with the exception of brief passages quoted by a reviewer in a newspaper or magazine.

Black Rose Books No. Z240
Hardcover ISBN: 1-55164-057-0 (bound)
Paperback ISBN: 1-55164-056-2 (pbk.)
Library of Congress No. 96-86102

Canadian Cataloguing in Publication Data

Samuel, Julian
  Into the European mirror: a work by Julian Samuel

  Includes bibliographical references and index.
  ISBN 1-55164-057-0 (bound)-
  ISBN 1-55164-056-2 (pbk.)

  1. Nationalism—Europe—History. 2. Ethnicity—Europe—History. I. Handa, Aruna II. Kipphoff, John III. Title.

JC311.S35 1997   940   C96-900670-5

Book design and layout: Aruna Handa
Cover design: Aruna Handa, John Kipphoff
Transcription: Julian Samuel, Frédrique LeGoff
Cover illlustration: detail from *Into the European Mirror*, by Julian Samuel, 1994
Financial assistance provided by Multicultural Programs of the Department of Canadian Heritage

	BLACK ROSE BOOKS	
C.P. 1258	250 Sonwil Drive	99 Wallis Road
Succ. Place du Parc	Buffalo, New York	London, E9 5LN
Montréal, Québec	14225 USA	England
H2W 2R3 Canada		

To order books in North America: (phone) 1-800-565-9523 (fax) 1-800-221-9985
In Europe: (phone) 081-986-485 (fax) 081-533-5821

Our Web Site address: http://www.web.net/blackrosebooks

A publication of the Institute of Policy Alternatives of Montréal (IPAM)
Printed in Canada

CONTENTS

foreword 9

introduction 13

INTO THE EUROPEAN MIRROR

transcript 31

reflections on the mirror

John Kipphoff interviews Julian Samuel 85

appendix a screenings of the trilogy 115

appendix b and the critics raved . . . 116

appendix c biography of julian samuel 118

appendix d filmography, videography
& public collections 120

bibliography 121

FOR PEGGY, SILVANA, UWE AND VIR

Thanks Julian Samuel, Gordon Martin, Eric Smith, Frédérique Le Goff, Kieren Beattie, Philipp Mainzer, Elisabeth Scheder-Bieschin, Max Kölbel, Jonathan Ewbank, Ian McLachlan, Ilke Braun, Juliana Weynerowski, Ritu Banerjee, Geneviève Weynerowski & Peter Wintonick. Thanks also to Dimitrios Roussopoulos, Linda Barton, Frances Slingerland & especially Darcelle Hall at Black Rose Books.

The European is a close reasoner; his statements of fact are devoid of any ambiguity; he is a natural logician, albeit he may not have studied logic; he is by nature sceptical and requires proof before he can accept the truth of any proposition; his trained intelligence works like a piece of mechanism. The mind of the Oriental, on the other hand, like his picturesque streets, is eminently wanting in symmetry. His reasoning is of the most slipshod description. Although the ancient Arabs acquired in a somewhat higher degree the science of dialectics, their descendants are singularly deficient in the logical faculty. They are often incapable of drawing the most obvious conclusions from any simple premises of which they may admit the truth. Endeavour to elicit a plain statement of facts from any ordinary Egyptian. His explanation will generally be lengthy, and wanting in lucidity. He will probably contradict himself half-a-dozen times before he has finished his story. He will often break down under the mildest process of cross-examination.

Evelyn Baring, Lord Cromer *Modern Egypt*

FOREWORD

This year, 1996, marks the hundredth anniversary of the first public exhibition of motion pictures in Canada.[1] The event took place in Montréal on Boulevard Saint Laurent, also known as the Main, a north/south running street which marks both a real and imaginary border in the minds of Montréalers — a border which separates the eastern, primarily francophone part of the city from the western, once primarily anglophone part of the city. Considered neutral territory, the Main has served as the first home for many of Montréal's newest immigrant populations: Eastern Europeans, Italians and Portuguese, among others.

It is ironic that at the beginning of this century, the first films made in Canada were government-produced promotional advertisements to encourage settlers, while toward the end of this century, *Disparaître,* produced by the National Film Board, warns of the tripartite threat posed by declining birth rates, the encirclement of Québec by anglo culture, *and* the increasing numbers of immigrants, "foreigners", within Québec's borders. It was between two referenda on the issue of Québec's separation from Canada, in a nationalist, xenophobic and alarmist climate that *Into the European Mirror* enjoyed its Canadian première at Cinéma Parallèle on Boulevard Saint Laurent on February 20, 1994, nearly one hundred years after the Canadian début of motion pictures on the Main.

introduction to the european mirror

The publication of the transcript of Julian Samuel's *Into the European Mirror* on this hundredth anniversary is fitting in that the videotape explores (in English and French) the themes of real and imaginary borders, expulsions, nationalisms and identities — a timely achievement given that we are day by day experiencing what Homi Bhabha calls "the working out of a colonial dynamic:" the bombing of South Lebanon, war in Chechnya, the on-again, off-again ceasefire in Northern Ireland, hostage-taking and insurgency in Kashmir, sovereignty referenda in Québec and armed standoffs at native reserves throughout Canada.

Into The European Mirror is the second tape of a trilogy. What follows is a brief description of each of the tapes.

The Raft of the Medusa: five voices on colonies, nations and histories (1993),[2] the first tape of Samuel's trilogy is broad in scope and includes considerations of contemporary and historical views of emergent nationalism (British India and its partition in 1947), integration (Hong Kong with mainland China), and the clash between Occidental globalism and Islamic fundamentalism. These issues are connected to the phenomenon of twentieth-century mass migrations and the mechanisms underpinning history-making and postcolonial and emergent literatures. Interviewees in *The Raft* are Ackbar Abbas, commentator on Walter Benjamin and Hong Kong cinema, Thierry Hentsch, author of *Imagining the Middle East,* Amin Maalouf, author of *Léon l'africain,* Marlene Nourbese Philip, author of *Looking for Livingstone* and *Frontiers* and Sara Suleri, author of *The Rhetoric of English India.*

The Raft serves as the departure point for Samuel's investigation into the idea that the Occident has come to define itself in relation to Oriental cultures. *Into the European Mirror* includes a discussion of Occidental modernity and how both the idea of 'nation' and the production of national cultures are often connected to the identification, exclusion and expulsion of minorities, of "others". *Into the European Mirror* is a work on imaginary and real frontiers, expulsion and resistance, from the last Muslim Empire in Spain to Damascus, Palestine and London. In addition to a continuation of his earlier discussion with Thierry Hentsch, Samuel interviews writer Homi Bhabha, author of *Nation and Narration*, Dr. Chris Giannou, author of *Besieged: A Doctor's Story of Life and Death in Beirut* and Rana Kabbani, author of *Letter to Christendom*.

City of the Dead and the World Exhibitions (1995) concludes the trilogy. Samuel expands on the themes of the previous two videos by examining the extent to which beliefs inform architecture and monuments and how monuments in turn influence beliefs. Samuel examines the role of architecture in the gender and ethnic segregation of the pre-colonial, colonial and contemporary Islamic city. He also canvasses the late nineteenth-century world exhibitions and their depictions of Egypt as a dirty, backward, disorganized place for their influence on late twentieth-century characterizations of the Islamic world. The rise of anti-Western sentiments in response to Western prejudices is also analysed through interviews with Former Egyptian Ambassador to the USSR and Algeria, Hussein Ahmed Amin, Edward al-Kharrat, author of *The Girls of Alexandria*, Max Rodenbeck, author of *Egypt from the Air*, urbanist Janet Abu-Lughod, author of *Before European Hegemony: The World System, 1250-1350*, author Timothy Mitchell, *Colonising Egypt* and Akbar S. Ahmad, author of *Islam and Postmodernism*. Spliced with the interviews are black and white footage of the Algerian war of independence, nineteenth-century paintings and images of present-day Egypt.

Together the tapes cut through the complexities of postcolonial politics and theory in an original and undogmatic way. The ever-rising tide of nationalism in the post-Iron

11

Curtain political world as well as the much discussed notion of an imminent clash between Western and Islamic civilizations make the thematic issues considered in Samuel's trilogy all the more topical.

NOTES

[1] It was a demonstration on the same French Cinématographe, a combined camera/projector patented in France by the Lumière brothers of Lyons which had been used for the world's first projection of film in Paris six months earlier. The films showed included clips of a train arriving, a boat going out to sea, the Lumières playing cards, among others.

[2] Black Rose Books published the transcript along with commentaries. See bibliography.

INTRODUCTION

American foreign-policy critic, linguist and philosopher Noam Chomsky has repeatedly stated that his main reason for declining the majority of invitations to appear on television is that his ideas are not amenable to sound bites, to the pace of television. He prefers the more accommodating format of books and articles which afford him the opportunity to develop cogent arguments. For film and videomakers, one solution to this problem is to produce a lengthy documentary, providing sufficient time for the unfolding of complex arguments. Canadian film producers Peter Wintonick and Mark Achbar did this in their award-winning film on Chomsky, *Manufacturing Consent,* which runs for almost three hours. A second solution is to limit severely the scope of the arguments under consideration; we see this solution practised on television news panels every day. Montréal video producer Julian Samuel's approach represents a third, less common option: the video essay — a short, dense video, jammed full of speech, images and text. Taking the concepts of frontiers and borders as both a departure point and a unifying theme, Samuel explores the cultural dimensions of "Western" identity by asking his contributors from across various fields to comment on what he considers to be key moments in the historical evolution of the Occident/Orient dichotomy. From the Spanish

Reconquista to the "discovery of the New World", from the frontlines of late-twentieth-century war zones to Norman Tebbit's "cricket test" method, Samuel explores dimensions of Western cultural identity in a largely theoretical framework, connecting the cultural studies discourse usually confined to the academy with the real world of nationalism, expulsion and war. The result is a difficult but engaging trip into the subconscious of humankind, with abrupt shifts from what *Now Magazine* critic Cameron Bailey aptly calls "sprawling discourse" to "sprawling discourse".

As *Into the European Mirror* opens, historian Thierry Hentsch states:

> I think that every frontier is both real and imaginary and the Alhambra here in Granada is just such a place — a frontier that has undergone historical changes which have left both very tangible traces, like the site on which we are standing, as well as traces that exist only in the realm of the imagination.

Samuel's enquiry is about how the material and imaginary traces of historical events manifest themselves within each other, reflect or fail to be accurately reflected in the West's historical imaginations as well as in its dominant historical-political discourses. His concern, in part, is to investigate the role of such imaginary traces in the major events of global politics. What is the connection between the fifteenth-century description of the Castilian gentleman and the current demonization of Muslims? Is there any connection between the fifteenth-century expulsions of Arabs and Jews from Spain and the 1990s expulsions of Palestinians from Israel? Is expulsion a necessary process in a Nation-State's quest for self-definition? To what extent do discourses about the "other" contribute to an understanding of ourselves as well as of late-twentieth-century political constellations?

These questions seem to demand a textual response, but Samuel refrains from a straightforward textual delivery. Instead, he weaves his thesis with a blend of talking-head interviews, archival news-footage, new footage shot on location in Spain and elsewhere, and a myriad of juxtapositions of image with image, text with image, sound with image. Despite uttering only a few words of his own, he manages to deliver a powerful, complex and humourous tape, connecting a great number of topics which one would not usually see connected in a more conventional documentary.

Samuel's approach is a broad, thematic one, drawing on many cases of cultural identity construction and in particular raising questions about the Occident's lack of recognition of Islamic contributions to Western, read European, culture. His approach is not ostensibly personal. Samuel restricts himself to commenting on the presentation of his contributors' ideas, which hail largely from the world of academic theory. Canadian video producer Jayce Salloum, who deals with similar topics in his recent tapes *This is not Beirut (There was and there was not)* and *Up to the South,* invites the viewer to accompany him as he embarks on a journey through the ruins of a ravaged Beirut and remarks on his personal identity crisis as a Canadian of Lebanese origin. Salloum shares with the viewer the apprehensions and limits he encounters as he attempts to position himself and reframe the relationships, sites, subjects and views of particular geographical places and times in which the Orient and the Occident are entangled.

While Samuel does not invite us to share his own personal meanderings in the construction of his self-identity and instead treads comfortably on the theoretical ground broken by the first video of the trilogy, *The Raft of the Medusa*, the effects of boundaries, real and imagined, on the individual are explored to some extent in the interviews with doctor and writer Chris Giannou and critic Rana Kabbani. Giannou details his experiences as a doctor working in war zones for the Palestine Red Crescent Society:

> I have left the physical frontiers and borders, but I cannot leave the moral frontier/boundary of Shattila. That is something which remains with me. . . . What continues with me when I then go off to Cambodia or to Somalia or to Afghanistan to perform surgery is the moral boundary, the moral frontier defined largely by human dignity.

In a vein similar to that struck in the opening chapter of Edward Said's *Orientalism,* Damascus-born critic Rana Kabbani, detailing her experience of a visit to the Alhambra, relates the effects of her research into Muslim and European history:

> . . . it makes me feel that at least I can retain self-respect in Europe because my contribution as a Muslim and as an Arab to the formation of Europe has been immense. Even if it is a contribution that is unacknowledged by Europeans, it is still there.

In *Into the European Mirror,* Samuel also offers a critique of the conventions of documentary film-making by subverting a few of its standard tools, particularly those connected with guiding the audience: the voice-over, repetition, and the use of text to label images. Samuel's decision to allow the interviewees to speak for themselves without the provision of introductions, comments or explanations is a deliberate one. Interviews are not bridged with explanatory voice-overs, though a caption with the speaker's name appears along with the title of a recent publication. Samuel operates under the assumption that abrupt shifts permit a greater understanding of currents underpinning the making of history. These abrupt shifts are graphic reminders of the historical ruptures which are often smoothed over in the linear narratives of the hindsight-blessed historians of the hegemonic West.

Thus, although the tape is a highly disjunctive work, it is also possessed of thematic integrity. Exploiting, among others, the themes of the looking glass, frontiers, borders and identity creation, Samuel delivers his thesis, or rather, his thesis seeps out and is reinforced by the repetition of visual and aural motifs. It is not the image in isolation, nor the text, nor the sound track, but rather, it is their combination which convey his thesis that expulsions and national identity construction are connected. The expulsions of Muslims and Jews from Spain at the decline of the Muslim empire, urges Samuel, ought to be compared with the expulsions of Palestinians from the Occupied Territories at the end of the twentieth century. This unifying impulse behind expulsions of peoples: creating national identity by defining it against a backdrop of the "other" is explored in a variety of contexts. The determination of who is to be expelled marks the boundary between self and "other", as the expelled fulfill the function of a reverse looking glass to the image of the self.

The title *Into the European Mirror* was inspired by Hentsch's work *Imagining the Middle East*. In his review of Hentsch's book, Samuel writes:

> The Orient, Hentsch theorizes is the empire's reversed looking glass, always ready to reflect whatever response Europe wanted: Europe has democracy; the Orient has oligarchy and despotism; the Occident is feminist, the Moors practise female circumcision, etc.[1]

17

Kabbani takes up the looking glass theme in the tape when she proposes that the Castilian notion of an aristocratic gentleman is born from his desire to contrast himself with the Muslim merchant.

The subtlety of the thesis delivery is evident in Samuel's use of the aural motif of birds singing. Against a backdrop of a wall in a garden of the Alhambra, text appears on the screen detailing numbers of deportees in Canada in the 1990s — this to the sound track of birds singing, peaceful. The same sound track is heard again at the close of the tape when the viewer is treated to a black screen with tiny dots of light, periodically growing bright and then fading away: Baghdad under bombardment in 1991. The aural motif suggests that expulsions and war are points on a continuum — that solutions to the problem posed by the Oriental's presence in the Occident, or indeed posed by the omnipresent "other" remain to be found. The use of the motif poses the provocative question: are expulsion, war and genocide parts of the extensional definition of Orientalism?

A humourous example of Samuel's subversion of the text-explaining-image-convention is his combination of the archival footage of Yassar Arafat with the accompanying caption, "As Hegel says...". Before this image is screened, the viewer hears the voice of Thierry Hentsch explaining how the West recognizes the existence of periods that preceded the rise of the West only in so far as such periods helped pave the way for the emergence of "universal" Western civilization. While the image of Arafat shows on the screen, the voice of Hentsch is heard:

> As a result, an enormous portion of history, fully one thousand years, was bracketed off — a portion that of course includes the Arab-Muslim world, or more precisely, Arab-Muslim civilization. As Hegel would make clear

several centuries later, to the extent that this Arab-Muslim civilization did not — again according to the Western view of history — contribute to the emergence of the West, it is not taken into account; it is excluded from this "universal" historical current.

Samuel also subverts the voice-over tradition of documentaries by juxtaposing or emphasising the speech of his interviewees with images. Unlike the Mutual of Omaha voice-of-god narration in which the announcer is heard but never seen, the voice-over in Samuel's video is a departure from the on-camera interview. When the talking head disappears but the talk continues, Samuel contextualises and comments on the speech. Occasionally, he accomplishes this by simply departing from the talking head image of the interviewee and cutting to footage shot on site at the Alhambra. The viewer sees Hentsch speaking in the gateway to the fort and then, while the voice of Hentsch is heard elaborating on the imaginary traces, the camera reveals scenes of the palace, illustrating the material traces. Further along in the tape, as Hentsch relates the process of cultural homogenization of Spain carried out in part by means of the expulsions of the Jews and the Muslims, the viewer is treated to a medium shot of the fountain in the courtyard of the fort. As Hentsch proceeds to the story of the bloody genocide of the indigenous populations in New Spain, the water in the fountain turns red.

As it is for Said, Samuel's Orient is largely limited to what is in Europe and North America referred to as the Middle East. Much has been written about the problems associated with the use of terms "Orient" and "Occident", "Orientalism" and "The West". Wilhelm Halbfass, among others, has correctly pointed out that the emergence of America, Russia and Japan as protagonists of the modern world has changed the meaning of "East" and "West".[2]

19

Instead of clarifying the definitions of these terms, in his landmark book, *Orientalism,* Said added to the confusion by offering several inconsistent definitions of "Orient", "Orientalism" and "Orientalist". Aijaz Ahmad, among others, has recorded his objections to what he calls Said's "deeply flawed" book. Among the many objections levelled in Ahmad's rigorous critique of Said's thesis are the exclusion of the voices of those who are not members of the Western literary canon, the essentialising of the "West", and the ambiguity of Said's definitions of "Orientalism". Could Ahmad's criticisms be applied more or less unaltered to Samuel's work? In addition to a focus on the Middle East, Samuel's work shares with Said's both an interest in the reverse mirror function which the "Orient" performs for the "West" and a focus on representations of the Orient in European painting and literature. While Samuel does include the work of many contemporary critics and Said does not, I think that Ahmad's criticism of Said is overstated. He writes:

> What is remarkable is that with the exception of Said's own voice, the only voices we encounter in the book are precisely those of the very Western canonicity which, Said complains, has always silenced the Orient.[3]

While it is true that Said combs the Western canon for portrayals of the Orient and contributions to the Orientalist discourse, it is also hardly surprising. In order to pursue his thesis, the Western canon is necessarily the material to examine for Western portrayals of the Orient. What Ahmad objects to is Said's exclusion of the criticisms of other critics of Orientalism and especially his failure to mention them and the debt he owes them. This criticism of Said has been made by others, and in his paper, "Orientalism Reconsidered", Said attempts to redress the omission.

With regard to the accusations of essentialising the West and being ambiguous in the intensional and extensional definitions of the Orient and related cognates, neither Samuel nor Said in *Orientalism* delivers the definitive answer, though each uses the term without hesitation. The sort of specificity which Ahmad and others demand is perhaps impossible to deliver for one caught in the contradiction of wanting to disprove what he considers to be a perceptual distortion within a nonetheless dominant discourse. In order to do so he has to first engage with the position he opposes on its territory and terms and thereby contribute to its historical manifestation. To define once and for all "Occident/Orient", "West/East" does not address the problem that these and other related dichotomies, over the centuries — in a case of fiction being more real than reality — have become part of popular, individual and collective imaginations and thus permit multiple definitions.

In *Into the European Mirror,* Samuel is at great pains to emphasize that for him the Orient denoted by "Orientalism" is not simply demarcated by lines on a map but also, perhaps with more devastating effects, lines in the imagination. Close-ups of maps form one of many visual motifs Samuel employs to communicate his thesis.

While Chris Giannou describes the arms bazaars which spring up on disputed borders, or cause borders to be disputed, the camera closes in on a map of the Middle East and Africa. The focus fades and sharpens as the camera tracks the borders on the pre-decolonisation era map. When Samuel does broach some of the more gruesome material effects of borders he seldom supplies the expected images. Paradoxically, in these instances, his camera is shy. We do not see the Palestinian refugee camps inside the borders of Lebanon; instead Samuel prefers shots of representations of these borders: maps.

Samuel's use of the video essay format is not without its drawbacks. Clarity is occasionally sacrificed in this tape, presumably in the interests of time. What does Giannou have in mind when he discusses the "frontier of universalism", "artificial" or "natural" borders? These phrases cry out for clarification, but Samuel is silent. The answers are not here; although, like a page in a hypertext document, the tape is rich with links directing the viewer to other works (which might provide the answers).

Samuel does not feel obliged to provide counter-arguments, or to explore the obvious question of what happened to the pre-Islamic culture when Umayyad power established itself in Spain. One is not entirely sure whether he stands in complete agreement with each of his interviewees. His positions on the issues are not verbally articulated, they are hinted at visually. Images are more informative but at the same time less precise than text. Does Samuel agree with Kabbani who suggests that Catholic architecture is aggressive, phallic, dark and oppressive while Islamic architecture is gentle, light and unoppressive? By the time Kabbani's comments are aired in the tape, Hentsch has already made this suggestion in a categorically qualified manner:

> To truly appreciate Chartres, you have to spend a lot of time in the shadows. On the other hand, when you visit the Umayyad mosque in Damascus, you find yourself in the midst of light that is used in a completely different way. Dazzling light shines right into the courtyard of the mosque, completely engulfing those inside . . . . it has always seemed to me that mosques are much more open places than churches. I do not mean to suggest that one is a better place to meditate in than the other: each has its merits.

Hentsch's point is cautiously made. Why then does Samuel bother to lead Kabbani into an unqualified and stronger reiteration? While the inclusion of Hentsch's comments, which appear earlier in the tape, give food for thought, the inclusion of Kabbani's mar the argument by overstating the matter with the somewhat gratuitous but comical reference to the phallic oppressiveness of Christian architecture.

It is not news that frontiers and borders are at times the locales of acrimony and conflict which occasionally result in hostilities. It is not news that history is written by the victors. It is not news that some Western historians read everything which preceded the Occidental ascendancy as only an evolutionary prologue to the well-deserved universal hegemony of the West. It is not news that the self is often defined at the moment that the "other" is identified. What is novel is to hear these ideas articulated by historians, literary critics, doctors and intellectuals in the context of a video essay. The disjunctive treatment of these ideas in the context of the video essay is Samuel's innovation. Samuel disparages the cachet of innovation though:

> 'Radical' innovations happen every time a young, postmodern, cultural studies kind of filmmaker gets a write-up in any one of the politically inconsequential magazines that are supposed to overthrow patriarchy next Sunday at city hall. 'Radical' innovation also takes place every time an educated minority, including gendered minorities, put pen to paper, light to film or tape. It's just the same old thing in a different condom.[4]

In recent years, the independent film and video documentary industry in Canada has experienced a technological boon: Hi8 technology permits the production of a tape for a

23

small fraction of the costs associated with film and Betacam SP video production. Hi8 technology has permitted both a broadening of the scope of subject matter and a greater variety of approaches in independent video production. What the technology has not yet managed to provide is a solution to the crucial issue of distribution.

Samuel identifies distribution as the number one difficulty facing independent documentary producers who are unwilling to compromise their work to suit existing "industry standards". Wide exposure at film festivals, air time on national networks, and inclusion in the public collections eludes the work of many independent producers working in Canada and elsewhere.

Samuel does not take rejection lightly. He is known to request itemized lists of reasons for rejections, and he has developed a number of theories about the arguments dictating his exclusion from national television networks and public collections. He cites the "mind-candy mentality of TV producers who are even worse than film studies and communications professors" who fear "documentaries that manufacture questions."[5] Samuel maintains that: "TV programmers in this country underestimate their audiences and try to protect them from the world of difficult ideas."[6]

At an Ontario television station, the Administrative Coordinator for Documentaries reported that she found Samuel's work "too dense", that she had to rewind sections of it to "better understand its complexities" and that she could not consider airing it unless it were divided into twenty parts with voice-over bridging. Queries Samuel: "One wonders what is too dense? My tape? Or her?"[7] In an interview with Toronto *Now* magazine's Cameron Bailey, Samuel conceded the point, but he added, "I think one should be tolerant of documentaries that are a little too dense for their own good."[8]

Samuel does not stand alone in this struggle. Peter Wintonick's and Mark Achbar's documentary film, *Manufacturing Consent,* about Noam Chomsky and his ideas on media and politics, also received a rather cool reception from the industry's bouncers. Initially, the Canadian Broadcasting Corporation (CBC) refused to air the award-winning film and only after a letter-writing campaign was mounted by its producers did the national broadcaster consent to air it with the stipulation that it be shortened. There is an appreciable measure of Canadian specificity in this regard: Channel Four (UK), TV Sweden, TV Portugal and Finnish TV aired the film in its original format and length.

Another oft-cited reason for rejection of Samuel's work is "sub-standard" production values where the "standard" is established by television broadcasters including CBC and the American networks who are ever mindful of ratings and the tastes of advertisers. It is true that the quality of Hi8 tape transferred to Beta is inferior to the more expensive, Betacam SP and digital technology; however, despite its inferior quality, Hi8 is broadcast on current affairs programmes, and many of the newer Canadian cable channels, including the Women's Channel, do broadcast independent productions shot on Hi8 video.

Samuel adamantly defends his artistic values including the production values of his recent tapes. Given the opportunity, he argues strenuously that every special effect, camera angle and lighting technique is deliberate. He shuns the "sanitized" look of the majority of made-for-television documentaries. We know these programmes: the establishing shot, the earnest, reassuring woman's voice-over, or else, an "objective" Peter Ustinovian baritone identifying for us what we are seeing, explaining the images, spoon-feeding us the message. There is not much content and what little there is is repeated several times throughout the

25

programme to ensure that the viewer does not get lost. We have seen these documentaries though only occasionally do we watch them on our televisions — these are programmes to fall asleep by.

Samuel's production values by contrast invite the viewer to engage with the tapes on a more intimate level. The space between producer and viewer is bridged somewhat by Samuel's rejection of the sanitized look. The viewer is encouraged to consider her own positions on the various issues raised in the tape: how would she handle similar considerations? Samuel's production values do not announce a complete, finished product ready for passive intravenous transmission; rather they connect his questioning approach and his content. The indirect miking of Samuel's voice as he poses a question to Hentsch reminds the viewer that this documentary is the work of a person, not that of a faceless corporation.

Samuel argues that he chooses the aesthetic precisely to criticise the existing standards of documentary format in which content is often compromised in favour of glossy production values and special effects clichés.

> It is counter-productive to make visually dazzling works that claim to be informative in the sense I need. The analytical structure could become too flimsy: the talking-head job is an essential ingredient for my work . . .[9]

It is not the case, however, that attention to content and high production values are mutually exclusive. Samuel's work would benefit from greater precision in terms of camera angles, quality of special effects and details. One gets the impression that Samuel is impatient with his work, that he cannot be bothered to pay attention to detail. From misspellings in the credits and subtitles, to an inelegant translation of Thierry Hentsch's comments in the tape, Samuel cuts corners and the results are occasionally sloppy.

Attention to these details is often the work of one if not several individuals on a television production team. Julian Samuel is, as the credits of the tapes announce, jack of all trades: producer, director, cameraman, and much else besides including translator, researcher, publicist. Despite his repeated claims that money plays no role in his production values, I maintain that Samuel's work would benefit from a generous budget. At the première of *Raft of the Medusa*, Dr. Charles Acland introduced the tape with a comment that *The Raft* was made for about a tenth of a single segment of the CBC flagship news documentary programme Fifth Estate, the price tag of which is $200,000 on average. "More," whispered a Fifth Estate researcher sitting next to me in the small Cinéma Parallèle theatre. I argue and Samuel denies that his tapes would be significantly better with a Fifth Estate single segment budget. Samuel counters that he would rather make ten tapes for $200,000 than one with higher production values.

The problems of funding and distribution faced by most independent filmmakers are compounded when the filmmaker is a woman or a visible minority, and even further complicated when the subject of the documentary is controversial or beyond the limits of conventional debate. Samuel, though, resists the temptation to enter the debate on the lines of race. "Representational politics is boring, stupid, provincial, super-regional, anti-international, anti-intellectual race-gender-based crap."[10]

> If we start the critique at race, we'll end the critique at race — and we'll get nowhere. We've got to start the critique in international politics and revamp the whole fucking society. As romantic and naive as that sounds, I'm still involved in trying to do that.[11]

Samuel does not deny the impact of racism and sexism, but he insists that the race game be used only as a tactic and never as end in itself.

As has been mentioned, the tape has been described by one Canadian broadcasting company as too dense. It is, in fact, a dense tape. Unlike many made-for-television documentaries, *Into the European Mirror*'s pace often leaves the viewer intellectually breathless — but if this pace and this density are the weaknesses of Samuel's work, they are also its strengths.

In *Into the European Mirror*, Samuel challenges the viewer to consider the extent to which the tentacles of Orientalism shape our thoughts, inform the structures of our institutions, proscribe what is possible to imagine. Samuel suggests that what we are capable of imagining is delimited in part by the far reaching, over-arching system of thought known as "Orientalism". The insidiousness of the notion of invaded imaginations, of colonized minds and bodies has been a twentieth century preoccupation from Orwell's cautionary *1984* to the all too non-fictional accounts of American patenting of the DNA of not only certain American citizens, but also of members of indigenous communities throughout the world. While it is possible to read *Into the European Mirror* as a cautionary tale — it does after all end with beautiful and eerie images of the bombing of Baghdad — it is not the case that Samuel's prognosis is an altogether pessimistic one. The borders of our imaginations are thankfully malleable — they may be redrawn again and again.

NOTES

[1] Julian Samuel, "West chided for its view of Mideast," *The Gazette*, Montréal, Jan 16, 1993:J3.
[2] Wilhelm Halbfass, *India and Europe*, (Delhi: Motilal Banarsidass, rpt 1990, 1988) p.160.

³ Aijaz Ahmad, "Orientalism and After," *In Theory*, (Delhi: Oxford University Press, 1994), p.172.
⁴ See: *Reflections on the Mirror: Interview with Julian Samuel* in this volume.
⁵ Julian Samuel, Panel Discussion, John Spotton cinema, Toronto, June 11, 1994.
⁶ Ibid
⁷ Ibid.
⁸ Cameron Bailey, "Julian Samuel takes tottering system to the edge," *Now Magazine,* Toronto, June 16-22, 1994:51.
⁹ *Reflections on the Mirror: Interview with Julian Samuel* in this volume.
¹⁰ John Spotton Cinema.
¹¹ Bailey, 51.

INTO THE EUROPEAN MIRROR

(edited and abridged)

a video essay by
Julian Samuel

interviews with:
Homi Bhabha
Chris Giannou
Thierry Hentsch
Rana Kabbani

transcription: Julian Samuel, Frédérique Le Goff
translation of Thierry Hentsch: Gordon Martin

CHRIS GIANNOU
The Nation-State is an artificial and arbitrary model, which has been imposed on many societies whose human dimensions do not respond to the concept of the Nation-State. You have postcolonial Nation-States and post-imperial Nation-States confined within artificial borders and frontiers. Conflict is part of the consequence of such artificiality and arbitrariness — of the segmentation of large geographic areas into Nation-States. I have worked on frontiers largely because my type of work — war surgery — deals with those types of conflicts which end up in hostilities.

THIERRY HENTSCH
I think that every frontier is both real and imaginary and the Alhambra here in Granada is just such a place — a frontier that has undergone historical changes which have left both very tangible traces, like the site on which we are standing, as well as traces that exist only in the realm of the imagination.

What's interesting is that we regard this site, which was once Muslim, as an architectural curiosity, forgetting that is it not merely of architectural interest, but also bears the imprint of an entire civilization that once flourished here — a civilization without which modern Spain, and perhaps even Europe as we know it today, would not exist. It's also interesting that most

37

of the people who visit this real frontier — this architectural site — are probably unaware that the traces left behind are not just made of stone, but also inhabit the realm of the imagination. However, the impact of Muslim civilization on the European imagination has yet to be acknowledged; it has not been accepted as a positive force. Let me make myself clear: as much as those of us who visit this site appreciate Arab or Arab-Muslim architecture, which we still regard as beautiful, we refuse to recognize that our Arab heritage consists not only of this magnificent architecture, but also includes an entire body of science, an entire view of the world and an entire philosophy, which, since the Renaissance, we have bracketed off and placed in an enormous gap we call the Middle Ages. So, the Alhambra is perhaps a fitting place to begin to talk about the suppression of Arab influences and to attempt to demonstrate that this negation of the Arab contribution to European science is part of a specifically European view of history which fails to acknowledge that much of our heritage comes to us from the Arab world. This negation dates back to the Renaissance, when people began to work directly with Ancient Roman and Greek texts again, forgetting that before the revival of these texts, our knowledge of Greek philosophy and the scholarship of the Hellenic world came to us by way of Arab philosophy.

G I have worked for ten years with the Palestine Red Crescent Society because the Palestinians are the victims of a historical injustice. The Palestinians are the victims of victims. We have seen how the genocide of European Jews — by Europeans, while other Europeans stood by and just allowed it to happen, and then the victorious allies refused to take in large numbers of Jewish refugees from Europe, in effect, condemning them to their deaths — created such a complex of guilt and culpability in Western public opinion that to expiate this guilt, another people was victimized, in this case the Palestinians.

So there is a choice to be made. One can take care of the victims of both sides. I have been in situations as a doctor with the Palestine Red Crescent Society of risking my life under bombardment to take care of not only my Lebanese and Palestinian patients but also my Israeli patients, prisoners of war in the hands of the PLO [Palestinian Liberation Organisation]. As a doctor, I have no problem with taking care of Israelis or Lebanese or Palestinians or whomever, but there is a difference if I am to choose to work and thereby strengthen and reinforce the structures on one side rather than those on another side.

THIERRY HENTSCH Here in Granada, one history was driven out by another. Clearly, Arab or Muslim history was driven out by Spanish, Christian, European history. What is fundamental is that people were driven out along with their history. It's quite telling that shortly after the fall of Granada in 1492, Spain began expelling Jews, and then, several decades later, Muslims. So once again, not only was a history supplanted, so too were people and a way of thinking — a culture — because those who seek to exclude the "other" inevitably restrict their own universe. It is important to remember, however, that during the Muslim era in Spain, which lasted approximately seven centuries, the three religions Islam, Judaism and Christianity existed side by side. And for much of what is referred to, either rightly or wrongly, as the Spanish reconquest — the Reconquista — Aragonese and Castilian monarchs continued to allow the three religions to coexist. It wasn't until the Reconquista was complete that the "other" ceased to hold any attraction whatsoever. Only then could the "other" be entirely dispensed with; only then could the entire country be brought under control and dominated by a single culture.

This is perhaps what is most tragic about Spanish history: that an extremely rich and diverse country, where several cultures had coexisted for centuries, made the curious decision to close itself off from foreign cultures, or rather "other" cultures and that it did so just as the Renaissance was beginning to take hold, at the very moment when what would come to be known as Western civilization began to define itself, extend its reach and export its view of the world. So what is most unfortunate about the process of exclusion that began to characterize this civilization as of 1492 is that it was exported overseas. The process of exclusion itself was exported to the countries we now refer to as Latin American, where, as we know all too well, the native "Indian" populations — the members of the great Inca and Aztec civilizations — were excluded from that part of the world they once called home. It is perhaps no coincidence, then, that Granada was recaptured in 1492, the very year Christopher Columbus landed on the shores of what he thought was Occidental India, which was in fact the continent that would become known as America.

CHRIS GIANNOU In my book, *Besieged: A Doctor's Story of Life and Death in Beirut,* I end with writing about the time when I left the Palestinian refugee camp of Shatila. I have left the physical frontiers and borders, but I cannot leave the moral frontier of Shatila. That is something which remains with me. Frontiers also delimit a moral space — a space of values which perhaps were engendered before Shatila, but were perfected in Shatila, were nuanced in Shatila, in my experiences with the refugees of the Palestinian refugee camp under siege. It goes on and I find myself

Ragheb Ziad Ragheb Adjaj, 18

Raed Yusef Abdul Qader Zorub, 19

Hatem Yaqin Yacoub Muhtaseb, 28

constantly refining that concept and those values. What remains with me when I then go off to Cambodia or to Somalia or to Afghanistan to perform surgery is the moral boundary, the moral frontier defined largely by human dignity.

Shatila is a refugee camp of very ordinary people: carpenters, masons, students and housewives, a very traditional sort of society — ordinary people who perform extraordinary deeds. There are Lebanese as well as Palestinians, Christians as well as Muslims, not to mention some foreign volunteers. What is important in Shatila is the sense of human solidarity that goes beyond any ethnicity or religious affiliation. This solidarity is based on principles. There is a cause and that cause allows people to resist bombardment, siege and starvation, political oppression and blackmail — and, it allows people to maintain their dignity. Shatila is not unique. We have seen this resistance before in history: in the Warsaw ghetto, during the battle of Stalingrad, in Hanoi under bombardment, in the Soweto township in 1976. People maintain their human dignity and define moral frontiers through their struggle, and although each one of these events is a particular incident in a very, very long history of struggle, each has universal value. It is that frontier of universalism that I believe is defined by these various particular incidents.

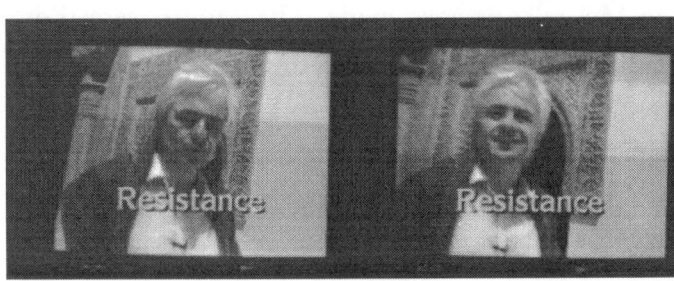

TH Of course, these expulsions [of Jews and Muslims from Spain] met with some resistance, but it is also important to note that they were carried out at a time when the Muslim world exerted little political influence. The Ottoman Empire was gaining ground east of the Mediterranean, but it did not yet wield sufficient power in the Mediterranean to lend real support to any demands the Moors may have made. The Moors were those people who had remained profoundly Muslim despite having been hastily converted to Christianity; they were, moreover, suspected of being bad Christians, just as the Jews had been before them. And some of them resisted expulsion. Force was undoubtedly involved in the expulsion of these people; they did not leave voluntarily. Their departures were difficult, sometimes very brutal, and in certain cases, clearly fatal. Some of those who were expelled were in such poor health that they did not survive the journeys they were compelled to make. So, they didn't put up much of a fight. They were not in a position to strenuously resist expulsion because the Muslim communities that remained in Spain were no match for the new Spanish regime.

JULIAN SAMUEL What brought about the fall of the Caliphate of Córdoba?

TH Oh! That I do not know.

Modernity and the fall of the Califate of Cordoba

A view from London

RANA KABBANI

If you look at the history, you find that there was a very long lead-up to the fall [of the Caliphate of Córdoba]; it was not something that happened under a military onslaught. In a curious way, the 800 years of Muslim presence in Spain already contained the seed of its fall because of the fractious nature of the different Muslim principalities in Spain. As soon as they started warring among themselves, as soon as they started warring with North Africa, as soon as they started siding with the Catholics against each other, which often happened — that division contained the seeds of their downfall. I think they are probably the same seeds we see today in the Muslim countries.

JS Did the demise of Muslim Spain help to construct Occidental modernity?

 Completely so. I feel, that the minute Wa'abdullah — Boabdil, as he is known in English — handed over the sword of his defeat, that entailed the defeat of what Muslim Spain stood for. Muslim Spain was a sort of multi-ethnic and multi-religious society — an innovation. After all, it was on the borderline of Muslim reality — it was an outpost of Muslim ideas. As soon as that idea collapsed at the end of the Reconquista, you suddenly had a "European self" forming on the relics of that idea, appropriating many of the major themes of that Muslim contribution for itself, pretending that it had suddenly fashioned them out of nothing.

The relic from my enemy

THIERRY HENTSCH Allowing non-Christian communities to survive would have been tantamount to making the frontier manifest in the interior — like carrying a scar inside oneself. I think that one of the main reasons that Isabella and Ferdinand resorted to an extreme measure like expulsion was their fear — a fear obviously inspired by political concerns — that these communities would create problems for the Spanish State, which was in the process of consolidating its power and establishing itself. It's quite clear, then, that the Spanish State regarded homogenization as a source of strength — as a means of acquiring political power. And it's important to remember that the politics of the Spanish State were still very expansionist at this time, for it was during this same period that Spain made its colonial conquests on the other side of the Atlantic. Consequently, this homogenization was in some respects part of an effort to make Spain the spearhead of an Empire — to make Spain itself monolithic. And a monolith cannot be built without exclusion. But these political motives may conceal a more fundamental, more unseemly motive. In effect, allowing the Muslims and Jews to remain in Spain would have meant acknowledging that something came before us — that before we came to be, there was a civilization just as remarkable, if not more remarkable, than our own. And although there may have been a willingness to retain some material traces of this prior civilization, all traces of its culture, social practices and political structures had to be completely wiped out.

RANA KABBANI The Europeans saying: oh, this is absolutely wonderful and sophisticated and superb and complicated and I can't possibly say that I've taken this from somewhere else — I have to say that I made this. It's not the relic from my enemy, from the Muslim, the Arab and the Spaniard who had embraced this culture and thus were the enemy of the Reconquista mind. I can't possibly admit that my heritage is from another culture which I despise.

Some of the great clashes of cultures in history — not just modern history — have dealt with arms, weaponry and the forces of destruction: that is, not just with the technology but also with different tactics. As a result, frontiers have always become arms bazaars. One culture has only bronze weapons and another has iron weapons, as in the Hyksos invasion of the Middle East and of Egypt; it is obvious that the iron tools, the weapons superior in technology, will then be taken up by the other culture, eventually. We see the same thing with the Macedonian Phalanx, a tactic which allows a very small Greek force to overcome a huge, imperial Persian force. There you have the other culture taking up the new tactics.

What I think is different in contemporary history is that in the beginning of the twentieth century we in effect no longer have any new frontiers in the world — in the

55

sense of a pushing-out of one culture or another. The world is colonized, the real frontier of the twentieth century then becomes outer space. What we then have is a globalization of many contradictions, including the weapons trade. It is no longer a question of weapons or military tactics being taken up by one culture copying another. Instead we have a fully developed industry and commerce. Countries that are totally incapable of producing sophisticated weaponry are quite capable of buying it. I think this is quite new in history. It means that destructive power has been universalized. It is very easy to ship across the oceans a supersonic airplane, heavy artillery as well as the technicians who will take care of it, who will maintain it and who will train other people to maintain this weaponry. It creates a dependence that was not there in the past. When you take up iron weapons you have to find a source of energy, coal, what have you, and iron deposits, which are present throughout the world. You can make your own iron weapons once you know how to smelt iron — the technology is relatively simple. But when you depend for your weaponry upon very sophisticated machinery, you cannot produce the spare parts, and as a result there is created a situation of almost eternal dependency in order to keep the weaponry functioning. It is perhaps this end of new frontiers as we have known them throughout history that has allowed the arms bazaar to be universalized. There is an international black market in weaponry where you can buy just about anything you want short of nuclear weapons. With the implosion of the Soviet Union, maybe even nuclear artillery shells will be available soon on the international black market.

JS That would make your job very, very hard?

CHRIS GIANNOU Nuclear weapons? No, because there would be very few people actually left to perform surgery on and there is not much you can do for people who have suffered massive radiation injury. What it means is that even in conflict zones where there is an artificial border — a frontier between two Nation-States, even if the State has collapsed — what you find is a commerce of weaponry that abides no ideology. One of the best examples is Lebanon, where each of the factions who were allied or at war with one another could buy weapons from the same arms dealers. It was simply a question of how much money you had. Some factions have access to other weapons sources, but there was a weapons market in Lebanon where anybody with money, whatever their ideological or religious bent, could furnish themselves with weaponry.

After ten years of war in Afghanistan, I think you would find the same thing in Central Asia, with the Soviet Union pouring in weaponry on one side and the United States and its various allies pouring in

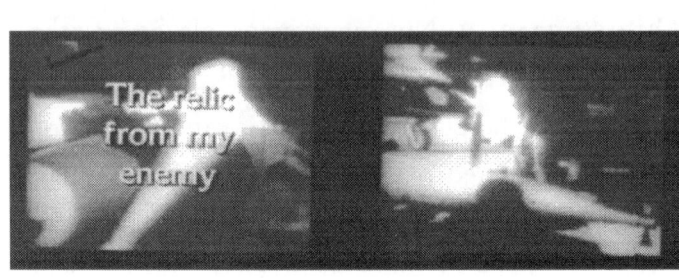

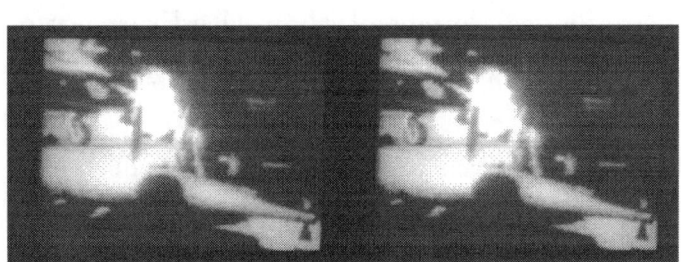

weaponry on the other side. A huge arms market was created with many of the weapons then finding their way to other war zones, through the international market.

Take the present conflict in the ex-Yugoslavia: Yugoslavia produces quite a lot of weapons, and you find Serbia and Montenegro exporting weapons even while they're in conflict as a means of gaining hard currency to continue their war effort within the ex-Yugoslavia.

So, frontiers in the twentieth century, borders, have become opportunities for arms bazaars. We certainly did not need borders to have the weapons market develop as it has, but at the verge of the 21st century, the three biggest industries in the world are weaponry, drugs, and religion.

JULIAN SAMUEL What does the Alhambra symbolize for you now as you look back at 1492?

RANA KABBANI I'll tell you a little story. I found it very difficult to go to Andalucía; I found it very difficult to travel to Granada. I come from Damascus. I am actually descended from the same line from which 'Abd al-Rahman is descended; my mother's family came back to Syria after 1492. When I went there and entered the Alhambra, I actually wept — I felt physically unable to tolerate the spectacle and there was an old guy, a Spaniard, a lame man, who came and sat next to me — my Spanish was rudimentary at that stage — and he asked me, "Where are you from?" I said, "Damascus," and he said, "Ah!" He understood why I had been overcome.

To see it now makes me feel two things; it makes me feel that at least I can retain self-respect in Europe because my contribution as a Muslim and as an Arab to the formation of Europe has been immense. Even if it is a contribution that is unacknowledged by Europeans, it is still there. The other thing it makes me feel is how a glorious past is often followed by a miserable present, and that is the state of the Muslim world at the moment.

JS Is it possible to connect the expulsions of the Palestinians now and the expulsions in Spain then?

THIERRY HENTSCH As long as you are careful not to distort the situation by making statements like, "So there you have it, exactly the same thing is happening again." I think that this comparison is interesting because it allows us to assess the extent to which these two phenomena result from a single state of mind. And I would identify this particular state of mind as the one that started to develop during the Renaissance in what would become the West, or Western Europe.

Arabo-Muslim history has been driven away by Spanish European Christian history.

What is particular to the Western world is the ideology that accompanies the phenomenon of exclusion: an exclusion prescribed by a universal ideology.

Every civilization relies on exclusion; every civilization tends to reject anything it doesn't want or anything it can't assimilate. So exclusion is perhaps not unique to the West. But what is unique to the West is the ideology that accompanies the phenomenon of exclusion, or in other words, exclusion that is justified by a universal ideology. The problem with the West is that it excludes in the name of a universal view of history, which recognizes the existence of periods that preceded the rise of the West only in so far as they helped pave the way for the emergence of this universal Western civilization. This view of history begins with the Renaissance; in fact, it became possible only after the Renaissance was underway — after the people of this period had rediscovered Antiquity and had consequently started to discount, or exclude, the Middle Ages. The Middle Ages was, after all, an invention of the Renaissance. As a result, an enormous portion of history, fully one thousand years, was bracketed off — a portion that of course includes the Arab-Muslim world, or more precisely, Arab-Muslim civilization. As Hegel would make clear several centuries later, to the extent that this Arab-Muslim civilization did not — again according to the Western view of history — contribute to the emergence of the West, it is not taken into account; it is excluded from this "universal" historical current. And this is an incredible historical outrage, an incredible act of historical exclusion, because it is quite clear that the Renaissance would never have taken place, or would not at any rate have developed in the way that it did, without the enormous scientific and philosophical contributions Arabs made to the Europe of the Middle Ages — a period during which, it is important to note, Arab civilization was at its height, as this site so clearly attests.

So to the extent that an entire portion of the history of humanity — in this case, Arab-Muslim history — is not considered to be part of the universal flow of history, this civilization has been excluded. And I think that the initial attempts to exclude the Palestinians are an illustration of this. For example, this exclusion is expressed in very concrete political terms in a memorandum that Lord Balfour sent to Prime Minister Lloyd George in 1919, which can be paraphrased as follows: "Of course, by instituting, by implementing the Balfour Declaration in Palestine, we are denying the rights of the country's Arab inhabitants. But these rights are much less important than our historical ties with this part of the world." Balfour does not, in fact, use the term "historical ties", but rather the word "Judaism". He says that Judaism, or the fate of Judaism, is ultimately far more important than the fate of the inhabitants of this region. Why? Because the West credits Judaism, or more precisely, the writings contained in the Bible, with having contributed to its development. So what really motivated non-Jews like Balfour to implement the Zionist

1492
EXPULSIONS
1993

project, or rather to garner British support for the implementation of the Zionist project, was not concern about the fate of the Jews. This had absolutely nothing do with their involvement. Their concern was to ensure, by supporting the Jews if necessary, that the West regained a firm grip on what was regarded as part of Western civilization: i.e., the Scriptures, the history of the people of Israel and more generally, the history of the entire region now referred to as the Near East — which I prefer to call the Eastern Mediterranean — before the rise of Greek civilization. The emergence of Ancient Greece is regarded as a stage, or rather one more step, in the movement of history towards the West, but it is also quite obvious that in so far as the great civilizations of Antiquity are credited with having laid the groundwork for this step, they too belong to us. Clearly, supporting Judaism, and above all supporting Zionist claims in this region, is our way of laying claim to all that has happened in this region throughout history.

H O M I   B H A B H A

The notion of an internal foreign body, the minority, quite apart from the other territory that flanks your frontier has always been crucial to the nation. Think about it like this: every democratic nation — I assume we are talking about democratic nations or nations as constituted within the discourse of democracy, because we have other ways of describing totalitarian nations: we call them empires, evil empires or totalitarian States — will want to have some kind of monitoring civil rights body.

You have to recognize the minority within the nation in order to be a nation — you almost have to do it. The interesting thing, therefore, is to try and understand which time, which cultural temporality, which spatial position and which political recognition is given to this minority. This is a process within the construction — nation-building — of the outside-ness of the inside. The national boundary is not only that which keeps another country in its place but also that which defines the minority within [the nation].

An interesting subject which I have explored in my own writings on the nation is the double nature, the Janus-facedness, of the national boundary. The national boundary has always been constructed as a liminal reality within what is seen as the national body. So, at one time, insurgent miners in Britain were actually — could be seen in the late 1970s and the 1980s as — the enemy within. When the Tory government was trying to break the power of trade unionism in this country — which they more or less succeeded in doing during that bitter miners' strike — then the miners became the enemies within.

We are now moving towards a situation within Europe where political refugees and economic refugees, who are being used very often or who have been used as part of the labour force or who are the effects of much greater big-power geo-political negotiations, are soon going to have exactly that status of the foreign body or the enemy within.

RK All the concepts that we associate with European manhood and especially the ideal of European aristocratic manhood are those that formed in relationship with the Muslim, with the "other". For example, the idea of trade being despicable — that the aristocratic gentleman doesn't work — comes out of the Castilian notion of the Muslims as traders, as successful bourgeois. He [the aristocratic gentleman] has to be completely the opposite; therefore, he despises toil, he despises work, despises money. He despises all of the elaboration of the bourgeois notions which the Arabs introduce into Europe, in Spain.

So many things that actually form the European character: the notions of diplomacy, of negotiation, of travel-writing, of cuisine, of dieting, of medicine and of alternative medicine — all that we associate with modern European culture — come from that heritage, come directly from tenth-century Córdoba.

HOMI BHABHA When you begin to have Pakistanis or Nigerians or Afro-Caribbeans, standing in that place of minoritization or in that process of the nation's minoritization, then immediately the status of the outside-ness of the inside or the part of the whole becomes much more obvious, much more graphic. Now, at that point, there is a way of dealing with that issue by continually referring those populations back or giving them a genealogy — which I think is completely spurious — which returns them to their own nations. The result is one continually talks about Pakistanis in Britain, first generation, second generation, third generation, as if somehow they constitute the emergence of another nation into British sovereignty, into England. Of course this is absolutely not the historical genealogy by which the presence of Pakistanis or Asians or other postcolonial migrants should be read, because what they are representing is the working out of a colonial dynamic within the era of modernity. That is how they should be read. They are absolutely a part of the history of the great metropolitan, Western centers — a part unacknowledged or acknowledged only in a grudging and disavowing way for many years. This is why I think Rushdie speaks very appositely, in the *Satanic Verses,* when he says that the trouble with the English is that their history happened elsewhere — which is why they do not know what it is. The return of the migrant is precisely a recognition, a re-acknowledgement of the history of the West. But we continually have politicians faced with a spectacle of cheering Indians at an India vs. MCC [Marylebone Cricket Club] cricket match saying, "well, you know, if these people cheer for India, then somehow they haven't thrown their lot in with this country." In fact, this is exactly what Tebbit said; it is now known in the discourse of immigration as the "cricket test".

RANA KABBANI I am working on Muslim heritage in Europe — specifically that heritage which has not been included in the "official history".

JS To what sources are you going to go to excavate truths?

I do not think it is even a question of excavation; all one has to do is to try to introduce a kind of space for oneself as a minority that is not going to go away. I mean, what is going to be done with us? Are we going to be put in gas chambers? If we are not, if a final solution is not in the making for us — although I wonder about that after Bosnia — then we have to be digested into European life. We are Europeans. We have contributed to this continent and to its culture.

THIERRY HENTSCH I think that this is a good place to address this issue. Since we are here at the Alhambra, we can talk about Spain, but we are really talking about the West as a whole. Spain clearly relied on Arab civilization in order to create itself, but it also created itself in opposition to Islam and the Arab world. And that's why it is now so difficult for Spaniards, and Western Europeans in general, to acknowledge that the very civilization they defined themselves against is in fact a part of them — a part of Western Europeans. That's what makes the role played by the "other" in the construction of "otherness" so very ambiguous. We carry the rejected "other" inside ourselves. And it's precisely because this "otherness" remains inside of us that we continue to reject it so strenuously. For centuries, we have sought to minimize and even deny the important role played by Arab civilization in the creation of the West because we continue to refuse to see the "other" in ourselves. The "other" is what we reject. The "other" represents the negation of our identity. Acknowledging that this negation exists within ourselves would involve questioning in a rather radical way the very identity we ordinarily take for granted. I think that confronting the "otherness" within us would clearly force us to examine the components of our identity, and the notion of questioning our identity is obviously rather unsettling.

Canada: 4829 immigrants deported between 1 February and 31 July. Another 5000 targeted for expulsion by the end of 1993

The problem with identity is that we regard it as an acquired trait to be defended at all costs. This view of identity involves negation and the death of the "other". But identity can be something much richer and much more interesting than an acquired trait that is resistant to change; it can be a continual discovery, an ongoing discovery of the self and the multiple layers of which we are composed. And this more dynamic view of identity would clearly allow us to repair the broken link with the "other", who could then be seen not only as the embodiment of "otherness," but also as the embodiment of something we carry within ourselves — something that is part of us and contributes to the richness of our identity.

Chris Giannou The diversity of human experience is such that sometimes in my life I have felt as though my body were an allegory for what was happening in the world around me. When I first arrived in the West African nation of Mali, in 1968, I fell ill. There was an epidemic of cerebro-spinal meningitis. I was teaching at the time and one of my students fell ill and died of meningitis. I had malaria and then hepatitis, and in the middle of all of this there was a coup d'état and a radical nationalist regime was overthrown. Several months later, there was an attempt at a counter-coup d'état and the swirl of events seemed to take up my body, and those of the people around me in many cases, and it was almost as if the pathology of the individual were mirrored in the pathology of the society.

This mirroring is evident in other areas including Egypt, Somalia and Cambodia. In Cambodia, with millions of land mines scattered across the countryside, one looks at amputated patient after amputated patient — people who have stepped on land mines — and then you step back and you take a look at Cambodian society and you see that Cambodian society has been amputated. During the three and a half years of the Khmer Rouge regime, the Pol Pot regime, a whole sector of society basically disappeared. When the Vietnamese enter Cambodia in 1979, they find that there are only fifty doctors left in the country. They have survived because they have gone incognito. Immediately, half of them leave; so, a country of six million people has only twenty-five doctors.

In 1982, they open the medical faculty. In 1987, you have the first graduating class, whose members immediately become university professors — they have no clinical practice. But really, you begin from year zero; the society has to rebuild itself. I was there only two or three years later, in 1991, so I was working with Khmer colleagues who had been out of medical school for one or two years — they had no senior, experienced Cambodian doctors to teach them clinical practice. That whole generation had disappeared; they were dead or had fled the country. So you see Cambodia amputated. These young, medical professionals then have to take care of hundreds and thousands of peasants who go out into their fields, step on land mines and have their foot or leg blown away by the explosion. You see this amputation of individuals mirrored in the society. The sense of solidarity that exists in Cambodia is very, very restricted — it rarely extends beyond the nuclear family. In Cambodian society, you see an amputation even in terms of human solidarity.

JS Architecture, beliefs, monuments?

To the extent that monuments, and thus architecture, are an expression of faith, it is clear that they attest to the unique manner in which each society deals with the notion of transcendence. What has always struck me, in this respect, about Arab architecture, as opposed to Christian architecture — and by Christian I mean the Germanic-Roman architecture found in Western Europe, not Greco-Byzantine architecture — is that it is much less sombre than our architecture. We use light very sparingly. What do you notice when you visit Chartres, for example? You notice that the entire cathedral was to a certain extent — but only to a certain extent — constructed so as to draw attention to a particular kind of filtered light — light from the outside that is tinted by the stained-glass windows. To truly appreciate Chartres, you have to spend a lot of time in the shadows. On the other hand, when you visit the Umayyad mosque in Damascus, you find yourself in the midst of light that is used in a completely different way. Dazzling light shines right into the courtyard of the mosque, completely engulfing those inside. So, in some respects, the mosque appears to have been designed so as to ensure that we are exposed to the daylight; although, a certain amount of shaded space was of course set aside to serve as a refuge from the sun. But it has always seemed to me that mosques are much more open places than churches. I do not mean to suggest that one is a better place to meditate in than the other: each has its merits. I am merely saying that people do not meditate in the same way in dark, enclosed spaces with vaulted roofs as they do in spaces that are open to the sun, where they are in direct contact with the light.

RANA KABBANI The Umayyad mosque in Damascus is very intriguing for me. As a site, it narrates in its history the history of the city: the different religions and ethnic groups that lived in it. You have a Canaanite site, and then a Greek temple, and then a Roman temple, and then a Byzantine church, and then a Muslim mosque. This is unlike the experience of the mosque at Córdoba, where Catholicism imposes itself on this absolutely stunning field of columns — which in its essence is one of tolerance — and suddenly you have this grotesque structure of a cathedral rising in the midst of it, imposing itself in a very phallic, very aggressive way. In the Umayyad mosque you have a kind of continuation: it goes from the Greek mosaic to the Muslim minaret, to the Roman Basilica — it is a kind of almost pantheistic approach to architecture.

JULIAN SAMUEL The use of light in the church — how is it different from the use of light in the mosque that you've just mentioned?

RK In the mosque, you find the courtyard, where the sky with its natural light is part of the architecture, and the angle of the light is not in any way Baroque or threatening. In a cathedral, you find light filtering down from high above into the gloom and you have this shaft of light penetrating down — almost oppressive. I think the mosque, or at least the Umayyad mosque, has much more in common with Greek ideas of architecture on a human scale — architecture as something that uplifts man without threatening him.

The expulsions of 1492 set a pattern — a Western pattern — that is set and that we have not varied from at all, in Europe's relations with others, in its relations with colonies, and in its relations with Muslims in particular.

I do not see a difference after Bosnia, I do not see a difference between being a Muslim in fifteenth-century Europe and being a Muslim in twentieth-century Europe.

81

JS So it is ultimately very connectable?

RK Totally connectable: the idea of the "other", the stranger, the Muslim, the Arab, the Saracen, the Moor, the Jew, the Blackamoor — you do not like them, you're afraid of them, you despise them, you throw them out, or you burn them at the stake. There is no other solution: the European mind has still not come up with any philosophical solution. That is why we have a holocaust every few decades.

Producer, Director, Editor, Camera ....Julian Samuel
Banff Centre for the Arts Executive Producer ....Sara Diamond
On-line Editor ....Stuart M. Rankin
Post-production supervisor/Video Engineer .... Luke Van Dyk
Chyron .... Yau Ching
Audio Engineer .... Jan Levis
Audio Post-supervisor .... Paul Herspiegel
Computer graphic opening ....Stuart M. Rankin
translation (video) .... Natasha Pairaudeau & Julian Samuel

thanks

Homi Bhabha
Chris Giannou
Thierry Hentsch
Rana Kabbani
Charles Acland
John Akomfrah
Cameron Bailey
Mariella Borello
Jocelyne Doray
Amin Maalouf
Medical Aid for Palestine
Michael Dorland
Mona Fahmy
Bruce Ferguson
Leslie de Freitas
Richard Flint
Tomas Gardiner
Jesh Hanspal

Sean Kane
Nantha Kumar
National Archives of Canada
National Archives
Washington, D.C.
Patronato de la Alhambra
Y Generalife
Rocío Liñán Corrochano
Jerónimo P. González-Martín
Ian McLachlan
Fred Reed
Gayatri Chakravorty Spivak
Yeshim Ternar
Salimah Valiani
Arafaat Valiani
The Canada Council
Ministère des affairs culturelles
Banff Media Centre

made with the financial assistance of PRIM

for Erik and Chris

REFLECTIONS ON THE MIRROR

John Kipphoff interviews
Julian Samuel

*Raft of the Medusa:
Five Voices on colonies, nations & histories* (1993)
Into the European Mirror (1994)
City of the Dead & the World Exhibitions (1995)

JOHN KIPPHOFF What motivated you to produce this trilogy?

JULIAN SAMUEL This trilogy addresses the phenomenon of migration and how world views change when "outsiders" deeply alter the conventions of history to suit their own needs.

There have been and there will continue to be in the future mass migrations to the West with Third World populations situating themselves within the West: there is already a large population of Haitians inside Québec, Maghrebans inside France, Pakistanis in the United Kingdom, Turks inside German unified civility, to name just a few. Initially, the aim of this documentary was to foreground the narratives and debates that had been engendered by these situations but had not been widely listened to in the West.

The Raft of the Medusa was the departure point for the trilogy. The initial desire to make a straight-forward exposé of Third World literatures changed once I had conducted the interviews. The interviewees themselves enabled me to expand this project. The first part explains the frameworks behind the literature of "emergence" and gets at the motivations behind sceptical thinking about history. As this project progressed, I found myself documenting intellectual histories rather than simply excavating literatures which are in opposition to Western conventions.

Into the European Mirror follows the quest of *The Raft*, further developing a discussion of Occidental modernity and how the idea of nation is connected to the expulsion of peoples and populations.

After *The Raft* and *Into the European Mirror*, the next logical step was to take a look at the modern instruments of representation that Western civilisations have used to view others and project themselves. In the first two parts, there was a partial concern with the many historical methods of viewing the world. In *City of the Dead and the World Exhibitions*, I touch on how the newer tools of representation — film, photography, and the modern mass media — are used to present the historic and current Orient.

JK Why did you use the video and not the written format given that the work relies so heavily on talking heads anyway?

JS Any medium ought to be manipulated when attempting to present a debate that initially might have transpired in another medium. It is fun to take a medium which claims to be visual and to try to alter slightly its supposed role. Video is not strictly a visual medium, as your question implies. Just switch on the news and you'll notice that it is basically talking heads. The ten commandments initially written in stone are now available on CD-ROM.

I do use the talking head in a very persistent way, but this is not the complete picture. There are many visual passages that you may have ignored, or forgotten about, because the debates overall are embedded in interviews — but that's my fault.

That there are long passages in which one sees people being interviewed has much to do with my editing technique which uses what looks like — excuse the pretentious sounding claptrap — near-discoherence. In the trilogy, one sees thematic shifts which connect the ideas of one interview to those of another on what may seem like tenuous grounds — unconnectable paths, but this feeling of discoherence abates as the viewer gets used to the unconventional way in which the trilogy works.

JK So your work is innovative?

JS I use talking heads in a slightly innovative way. I can't make apologies for having long takes in which intellectuals explain complex ideas. The work is very anti-televisual. I am trying to pull in the audience by not using conventional voice-over bridging. To use voice-over is to assume that people need a guiding hand. The Canadian Broadcasting Corporation (CBC), a State organ, is addicted to using the voice-over bridge and, in my opinion commits the profound mistake of over-guiding audiences — this is morally wrong.

My work is not about to turn Western televisual aesthetics upside down. The world is overcome with formal innovation for misguided reasons. Innovation for innovation's sake is boring, empty and suicidal. Innovation emerges out of an honest admission that the old form one uses can no longer sustain the spectrum of needs demanded by a particular work at a particular time in history. Young intellectuals like to call this a "moment". It is only in retrospect that innovation looks more or less like a rupture.

The crux of the matter is that the analytical depth I achieve in the trilogy simply wouldn't work if I tried to embed these interviews in splendiferously rich, visually innovative passages. That meaningful poetry so frequently seen these days is desperately easy to construct. *Prospero's Books* by [British film director Peter] Greenaway is suffocating. There is no space and no time, just visually-poetically-correct moronic scene after scene.

It is counter-productive to make visually dazzling works that claim to be informative in the sense I need. The analytical structure could become too flimsy: the talking-head job is an essential ingredient for my work. Some radically innovative (innovative according to the prevailing winds in the Academy) filmmakers tell me that if I am so concerned with analytical depth, why not write a book or publish an article. My answer is quite simple: Black Rose Books is interested enough to publish a second book on my tapes. The trilogy is, to a large extent, about modern literature. I am manipulating an older medium in a newer one. Strange coincidence that a work which interviews writers finds itself inferring literature, is it not?

JK Structurally and aesthetically you consider your work to be "slightly innovative", but is it politically radical?

JS In a fundamental way this documentary is not a traditional work. This issue of what constitutes "radical" innovation or being a "radical" filmmaker is not something that keeps me up nights. I want to bring to the fore discussions that have been marginalised by the forces that be — by the preoccupations of conventional history-making and the not so nice militaristic corollaries that come with a particular educational formation. I try to address the blindness that is passed off as education without televisually spoon-feeding counter-arguments.

"Radical" innovations happen every time a young, postmodern, cultural studies kind of filmmaker gets a write-up in any one of the politically inconsequential magazines that are supposed to overthrow patriarchy next Sunday at city hall. "Radical" innovation also takes place every time an educated minority, including

91

gendered minorities, put pen to paper, light to film or tape. It's just the same old thing in a different condom.

JK What then is the difference between your trilogy and a conventional documentary?

JS My documentaries are different from those kilometres of socially nice films made at the National Film Board of Canada (NFB) by all those well-fed filmmakers who give me ulcers. These documentarists are always struggling (I don't know how anyone could struggle with those kinds of incomes and BMWs) to make things snappy and visual and poetic and ever so socially relevant.

CBC and NFB products are neither as well researched nor as analytical as my work — there may be a slight difference in "production values" — but this is a political question. CBC will show jerky super 8 footage when it has to do with the brutality of the commies and now, the fundamentalists, in Afghanistan, but it will only reluctantly deal with issues such as Montréal's weapons of death industry in our own backyard. In such a case, the argument of production values would hold supreme and a programme would not get aired. CBC looks conservative when one compares its programmes with the BBC's coverage of British investments in South Africa, or with Radio Netherlands' critical coverage of the Netherlands' expansionist history.

Though my work is low-budget, it is neither terribly radical — and, of course, that's for the critics to judge — nor very traditional. I've built an unpredictability into its very structure by editing it in a thematically disjunctive but thematically driven way. I am afraid this is a paradox, isn't it? Occasionally, this editing technique is plodding and desultory but I tend to resolve sections of discoherence with an overall coherence that unifies the entire trilogy along general thematic lines. It is, with a few blind spots here and there, a comprehensive treatment of how the intellectual West has looked at and used the Orient. I have not seen this done before on video or film.

JK What are the blind spots, and how does your disjunctive editing lead to an overall coherence?

JS Blind spots are those issues which I should have further developed. For example: the Islamic colonisation of Spain. As for the editing, you'll probably not believe me but, there is a great deal of pre-calculation of editorial events in the trilogy. I usually go through five or six, sometimes even seven rough assemblies before I get to the final on-line stage. The editorial manoeuvres are not coherent in the

93

conventional sense because a theme is not allowed to dominate a certain series of passages without being undercut by minor themes.

It is this lack of coherence and the only partial resolutions of questions which help create doubt about the form of the tape as an artifact itself and which reveals something about the culture in which it was produced. In this way, I hope to comment on and encourage scepticism about the production of histories.

JK Could you give a specific example of making connectable what is supposedly not connectable?

JS Yes, the use of layered imagery helps set a historical context for the talking head. In *The Raft of the Medusa,* when Amin Maalouf discusses heresy we see his mouth talking in the face of Archangel Gabriel. A little heresy on my part. I hope that I won't get killed — though I wouldn't mind the media attention. Also, when he concludes his "review" of religion, we are shown the inside of a religious institution. Immediately, Hentsch split-screens into this image of the institution and is tightly framed, almost suffocated, by the pillars. There he narrates how we construct "others" in order to know ourselves. I think by "ourselves" he means Europeans.

Throughout this trilogy, I have layered themes and images, for instance when I manipulate what generally have been referred to as "Orientalist" painters: Jean-Auguste-Dominique Ingrès, Jean-Léon Gérôme, Eugène Delacroix and Ludwig Deutsch, among others. These painters add the dimension of European pre-photographic perceptions of the Orient to the documentary. It is against the visual background of these Orientalist paintings that the interviews emerge as a review of the ways the European saw the Orient — an aspect more fully developed in *City of the Dead and the World Exhibitions*. These paintings also show how the world outside European civility was subsequently acted upon. Gerôme has projected the military arrogance of General Bonaparte in Cairo without framing the experience of "The Native" but Théodore Géricault's "The Raft of the Medusa" (1819) is an early instance of European sympathetic, reflective consciousness regarding the Third World.

I placed Gerôme's "The Moorish Bath" (1870) directly before Nourbese Philip's section in *The Raft*. Here, the theme of the painting is servitude. In this painting, a black slave is bathing a white woman — who herself may have been a slave. We leave this nineteenth-century construction behind when we cut to the forceful reflections of Nourbese Philip, a Caribbean-Canadian writer. I use this comparative approach of what the

95

perception of the Orient was just a few years ago to what it is now, as a minor theme in later stages of this work. I also contrast different ways the Arab world has been represented in Occidental media: I have squeezoomed over the earlier paintings Universal Newsreel footage of a Tunisian woman's fashion show; sandwiched in one frame paintings from the 1800s and film footage from the 1950s. There are also humble visual elements in the section with Maalouf: Gerôme's painting of Bonaparte in Cairo, for example, where I have cropped the details of his imperial balls in all their splendid, patriarchal rotundity.

Form and content merge in *Into the European Mirror,* when I scroll the names and ages of Palestinians killed by Israelis on Giannou's face while he talks about the horrors he encountered in the Palestinian refugee camp Shatila, in Lebanon. Obviously, these edits and montages are not radical innovations; they are just a method which is slightly off the beaten track and temporally makes comparable what is not or that which seemingly ought not to be compared.

Something similar happens with Thierry Hentsch, whose book *L'orient imaginaire* is a brilliant work. In it and on the tapes, he discusses Western history as myth-making. He asks how the Occident defines itself; he details how a collective "we" can only exist in relation to a collective "other". He goes on to show how this "other" is made up in the collective imagination of the Occident. His explanations splinter off into many directions. He interprets Delacroix's "The Death of Sardanapalus" as a way in which the West sees the Orient — pejoratively, of course. Subsequently, he offers a critical vision of CNN based on Géricault's nineteenth-century allegorical painting "The Raft of the Medusa".

So, I have brought together a critique of CNN with Gericault's painting of European guilt, and this co-mingling of things has much to do with what I try to achieve in this trilogy. I have done this kind of verbal to visual content comparison in *City of the Dead* as well — the visual overlays of the Egyptomania exhibition at the National Gallery of Canada in 1994 with the commentary of Timothy Mitchell on the world exhibitions of the nineteenth century.

JK I know that you consider the less than ample resources you had to work with an important factor shaping your work, possibly even a virtue or strength of it. Can you give me an idea of what went into the making of this trilogy in terms of funding, time and technical resources?

JS Funding is always a problem. Financial support for my kind of projects has always been miserly because there is no apparent high return, especially financially.

97

The importance of leaving aside financial considerations and enabling challenging works to be made is not obvious to most traditional funders. They are deathly reluctant to invest in my work. The Canada Council, after it was brought into alignment with contemporary race and representational politics, became a generous funder of my work. In the old days it was only the two white tribes who would get funding for the most moronic artsy-fartsy projects. The ultimate bore is that we don't have a Channel Four here as in England. We have only the conservative CBC.

I got the funding from the Canada Council, Multiculturalism and Heritage Canada and the Conseil des arts et des lettres. Here are the figures that went into making the entire trilogy: $30,000 for *The Raft*; $10,500 for *Into the European Mirror* plus $18,000 worth of on-line editing from The Banff Media Center in Alberta. Sara Diamond was my executive producer at Banff and is the best producer an experimental documentarist could dream of having. I put together $34,000 for *City of the Dead*. This makes for a grand total of $92,500. I produced this trilogy of 231 minutes duration between 1992 and 1995. My living expenses for those three years, too, came out of this grand total. I think my production record compares very favourably with that of the amply-paid, politically-correct filmmakers at the NFB and the CBC.

Even as a young filmmaker I was never good at getting funding. Believe me I did try, but I was always better at being boring and informative. It would appear that the more airy your project the more likely you are to get funding — at least that is the case in this country. Look at Québec. It helps if you're white and francophone as well. Look at how enormously superficial and merely illustrative *Le déclin de l'empire américain* is. And who could hold a candle to *Un zoo la nuit?* I could rant on and on but I'll leave that to Mordecai Richler.

JK Do you think that you have a difficult time getting funding because the issues you raise aren't ostensibly those that concern Canada or Québec directly?

JS The issues I raise concern Canada directly. My work is Canadian because these reflections on world history have been put into a visual form by a Pakistani-British-Canadian-Montréaler. What could be more Canadian than that?

The tapes are not about Louis Riel, nor are the issues about Québécois separatism, nor are the tapes about Canada's Group of Seven and whether these artists were early gay activists or not. Such Canadian issues I deal with in my novel, *Passage to Lahore*.

99

This trilogy is about the reflections of a more-or-less though not totally Canadian artist. Indeed I have, along with other Canadian writers and filmmakers, many belongings, and we ought to continue to resist being defined by any single, boring cultural parameter. We should reserve the right to comment on the worlds outside the borders of the countries or provinces we happen to inhabit.

JK How has the trilogy been received here in Canada and abroad?

JS The trilogy is not doing badly. It has been shown in a few festivals in Canada, nothing abroad as yet except a screening at the American University in Cairo. The philosophy department at McGill has shown it; the National Gallery of Canada has purchased *City of the Dead* with a view to including it in a show on something to do with postcoloniality, and the tapes are being used in classes here and there.

JK With hindsight, and had you had access to greater resources, what would you have done differently?

JS Would you have looked different if your mother had married a man from Côte d'Ivoire? Yes, things would have been different. Perhaps I could have bought a BMW like those CBC and NFB do-nothings. Anyway, the central focus would not have changed — a a few typos, in the subtitles etc., would have been eliminated by hiring a proof-reader, and I would have used a few more interview subjects. I also would have travelled to other relevant locations.

JK *Into the European Mirror* is concerned with the global hegemony of what are said to be Western concepts such as the Nation-State and the havoc these concepts have caused in the recently decolonised regions of the world. With your trilogy, are you seeking to debunk historically grown cultural prejudices in an academic exercise of sorts or are you more interested in indicting the States of the European Union, the United States and Canada for their continued misperception and exploitation of the non-Western world?

JS I am an independent filmmaker not a university professor; I cannot hope to address such a massive question in precise terms. And of course I don't want to be a Cultural Studies type and claim to understand all the complexities. My concerns are with taking apart myths around what you mentioned: global dominance, the Nation-State and so on.

The goal of the trilogy is to acquaint the viewer with the various fields of analysis — to make the arguments from different fields more comprehensible to an intelligent audience; not to vulgarize things but to make different conceptual frameworks applicable to one another.

JK Much of what you and your contributors say draws on ideas popularised by Edward Said in *Orientalism*. What do you make of the argument that Said himself practises essentialism with regard to the West, and do you not think that this criticism could equally be levelled at you? Might it not be more illuminating to disengage from this eurocentric cultural studies discourse and instead seek to illustrate the causes and effects of the rise of metropolitan capitalisms against the background of feudalist-dynastic politics and their connection to imperialist exploitation—especially for a recovering Marxist like you?

JS I am still convinced by a lot of what Marx wrote and I listen carefully to some intellectuals who have properly assimilated Marx. I don't at all think that Said is doing a great service to the Western powers. However, I am neither an expert on Marx, nor on Said. What does it matter in the grand scheme of things if Said is whatever he is? For me, he is a very necessary sceptic. For example on the current Palestine peace process he is extremely useful as a critic of the horrors of the PLO [Palestine Liberation Organisation] and their human rights abuses. As for the rise of metropolitan capitalisms, Marx gave all the standard answers to these questions — why are you bringing them up again?

JK It is not a question of answers which Marx may or may not have provided. Imperialism and the attendant issue of eurocentric historiography have not gone away, it's only that metropolises have been complemented and partly eclipsed in importance by the transnational corporations, as have issues of social justice by neo-liberal economics. Has it become impossible, at the supposed end of history, or in the supposed absence of any ideology which could pose a viable challenge to liberal capitalism, to create counter-histories? You seem to say that you have to be content with raising methodological questions about the construction of histories and encouraging a generalised form of sceptical thinking.

JS There is no end of history. That's just what the postmodern/cultural studies "theoreticians" and other self-promoting psychos say to get attention. Everyone knows they are as stupid as the universe is large, even with their nickel and dime doctorates.

A very learned friend, Michael Neumann, has suggested to me that Asian nations are just as autocentric about their historiography as anybody else. Massive cultures impose their values on weaker ones. Has Japan made much intellectual room to get itself raked over the coals? Ask others in the region. I'm not dead certain that the West has the perfect monopoly on autocentrism.

JK Aijaz Ahmad clearly disapproves of what he calls the psychologising impulse in Said's diagnosis that European identity rests on the construction and objectification of an Oriental "other". Are you merely making the humanistic point that we are all the same and that race and ethnicity are constructs of the divide-and-rule mind?

JS I am not deeply familiar with Said's psychological evaluation of the Orientalists' game. But generally I agree with Ahmad's very sensible and uncompromising critique of Said.

I think that Hentsch's review of *Orientalism* is apt: what Said does is thankfully not Foucauldian intellectual history. What he does, in *Orientalism,* is to list cultural and political complaints about the Western imperial powers. I don't remember much conceptual ingenuity there, but it is a book that has had a thunderous effect across university disciplines.

JK Why and how did you choose your contributors?

JS I research a particular area that I find fascinating, and I go the library and try to build up a general base of knowledge in the area, after which, in a general way, I take a particular position. If one develops too specific a knowledge, one can lose the big picture. An effective documentarist has to give a larger picture than does the particular individual whom he happens to be interviewing. I am trying to expose the big picture. But I can accomplish that only through a collation of the input of several so-called experts in the area. I think my trilogy is a good example of how voices from across various disciplines can deepen one's knowledge of history.

JK I ask because, and this ties in with my previous question, there is a certain thematic looseness, almost an arbitrariness in how the various contributions relate to one another. This looseness is in part responsible for making this video and the trilogy intellectually stimulating but it also opens you up to the criticism that the video lacks focus and that certain connections which are made are at best farfetched. For example, while it is a point worth thinking about, the connection between the 1492 expulsions of Jews and Moors from Spain and the 1993 deportations from Canada does not seem to me to be elucidated satisfactorily in *Into the European Mirror*. Do you claim—on the basis of your contributors' testimony—that with regard to those expulsions, Spanish-style identity politics are at work in the Canada of the 1990s?

JS I have been criticized for making the connection between Spain in 1492 and the expulsions of Palestinians in 1993 for all kinds of sensible reasons,

105

some of which I agree with. But my interviewee Thierry Hentsch actually answered this particular question with clarity and depth.

Canadian nationalism is not particularly strong. Here it is not as intense as in Spain in the 1400s. Then the driving force behind the expulsions was Catholic religious intolerance, economic competition and the idea, strongly supported by the papacy, that the Muslims must be stopped from taking over Europe and destroying the Christian faith. I don't really see a Canadian effort to define Canada's national character in these harsh terms. There are, of course, the headache-inducing constitutional conferences, the Meeches and Charlottetowns, and boring Québécois referenda which can be seen as nationalist projects. The latter I would call provincialism in the pejorative sense of the word; although, in Québec, things might indeed be moving toward the Spanish way of doing things.

JK For me, the video's strength — and at the same time, its weakness — lies in the use of very allusive metaphors such as surgery, frontiers, the relic of the enemy, etc. They anchor the various contributions and focus the viewer's imagination, especially as you superimpose these keywords onto the images at points of transition in the narrative, for example. On the other hand we get what seem like disconnected asides: Chris Giannou's analysis of the international weapons trade, how it needs borders, how it abides no ideology, etc. I suppose this is connected to identity politics and nationalisms without which we'd have no borders and thus, he seems to claim, no murderous weapons trade, but how exactly is this contribution connected thematically to your main concerns? When you reduce connections to a few keywords, almost anything can be made to look interconnected in an ahistorical, post-modernist sort-of-way. See the diverting asides on Islamic vs. Christian architecture and the former's (it is implied) symbolic openness as opposed to the latter's "oppressiveness". What are we supposed to deduce from this?

JS There is nothing postmodern about my work. I don't care about postmodernism — few serious analysts do. Postmodernists are well-dressed morons with no place to go.

There are no diversions in the trilogy — I tag concepts with the printed word on the screen because I want you to concentrate on a particular theme. There are minor themes that transpire throughout the work. For example, commentary on architecture permeates the entire trilogy. Take the connection between architectural commentary and Sara Suleri's discussion of binarism in the Raft: good and evil, colonial and not-so-colonial, black vs. white. I have merged this discussion with Ackbar

107

Abbas' comments on the politics and architecture of Hong Kong; the tenuous link is the establishing frame of the concept of binarism. When he discusses Hong Kong's absorption into China, he talks about countries moving at two different speeds and times — about the differing tactics of Chinese and Western architecture merging. These kinds of barely linkable content-entities are not commonly seen in documentaries.

JK You haven't quite answered my question, but let's move on. What is it about the fall of the Califate of Córdoba that makes you build *Into the European Mirror* around that particular history? Do you believe in the picture of a golden age of tolerance reigning there? Has the Muslim presence or have the expulsions from Spain been misrepresented historically? Why would you not for example choose multicultural Sarajevo or Mostar with its destroyed bridge as more timely symbols of pluralist culture destroyed?

JS Very good question. There have never been any tolerant regimes anywhere — as far as I know. This is a relative question that only the well-trained can answer.

About the second part of your question: I would have been scared to go into a war zone like ex-Yugoslavia. You need lots of experience to do this. I don't have it. I would have needed a crew of two or three with back-up equipment and I would have needed all kinds of official and unofficial clearances. Such a project requires a CBC or NFB budget; I would not have been able to look at this current situation in a meaningful way with my tiny budget. I also have the feeling that had I done it, I would have been so close to the fire that I might have been prevented from seeing the larger historical developments. However, my interview subjects do refer to this area several times to show the "universal" picture.

Actually, I really don't remember how I got to Spain. I think it was Maalouf's wonderful book, *Léon l'africain* (1986). Every part of this trilogy opened a path to the beginning of the next part. It just seemed logical to proceed with the expulsions of 1492 and to try to make the connection with what I saw as similar contemporary problems. Also, it seemed to me that if I were going to make something that would last that it would have to have near-discoherent connections in it. It is the seeming absurdity of comparing the Spanish Edict of Expulsion of 1492 with the expulsions of the Palestinians only a few hundred years later that made this intellectual exercise worthwhile.

JK When Thierry Hentsch discusses the role of alterity in the formation of (self-) identity, political, cultural or other, isn't he transposing models of twentieth-century nationalisms onto the feudal Spain of the fifteenth century?

109

JS You'll really have to ask him that one. However, I can give an amateur's answer. I suppose, by existing in the current century he is reviewing Spanish history from the vantage point of all the intellectual frames of looking at the past. Would you expect Issac Newton to comment on Einstein's theory of relativity, quantum mechanics, the concept of space-like separation, and computations that do not end? There are limits to the kind of question you are asking. One is locked into the analytical parameters of one's own epoch, with all the advantages and disadvantages this brings.

JK Aren't both Hentsch and Rana Kabbani overshooting somewhat, when they claim that Occidental modernity is constructed on the ruins of Muslim Spain? It's a pithy statement, but not as self-explanatory as they seem to think. With regard to the European appropriation of the ideas of Muslim Spain, be it notions about chivalry, nobility, the bourgeois, whatever, I feel tempted to ask Rana Kabbani, "and isn't it good the Muslims potty-trained the Europeans, before they had to leave for North Africa?" Can you concur with anything Rana Kabbani has to say, other than her personal sense of grievance? What about the remark about the "final solution in the making?"

JS Overshooting what? I agree with lots of what Rana Kabbani says. I think she is very direct and that is a relief these days with all the incoherent mess that is called intellectual life. Have you heard the way intellectuals talk these days? It is a joke! Read Baudrillard — now there's an inconsequential idiot if I ever saw one.

Since I am not a professional historian, I am not able to refute what Kabbani says. I am convinced that with what I see around me today — the way our media simplistically presents the horrid and complex situations in the world — that she is right. She is correct to say that Europe has a holocaust once every few decades.

JK Genocide and expulsion are for you typically European forms of behaviour?

JS All cultures carry out genocide. Genocide is the definition of culture — remember Walter Benjamin. There are nations that stand by and watch when this happens. Look at all of Europe standing by and watching as it happened in ex-Yugoslavia. In order to have genocide there has to be non-intervention from the rest of the world.

JK In spite of my scepticism about various aspects of the video, I think that it is a very imaginative way of introducing to the undernourished viewing public important concepts of and theories about histories, identities, nationalisms, postcolonialities, migrations, etc. Homi Bhabha's writings are largely unintelligible, but

111

his presence in this video is justified by one single remark (here slightly adapted): namely that the presence of Pakistani-British-Québécois-Canadians in Canada is merely the working out of the colonial dynamic. This and other statements might be considered banal by some, but I suspect that many among us have not ever been confronted with this very simple thought and its complications concerning — among others — immigration, multiculturalism. Is it your aim to popularise such ideas with this trilogy? If so, what can you do to make these subject matters even more accessible by gaining wider circulation for your videos?

JS First, thanks for the compliment. Popularise yes, vulgarize no. Bhabha is tricky. And one has to read his stuff over and over. Compare his writing with that of Montgomery Watt who is dealing with complex historical issues. Watt comes through in the first reading. Not Homi because he is somewhat obliged to talk the talk — it is the discipline he's in — but there are many original and incisive insights in his interview.

JK Can a largely historiographical exercise such as your trilogy shed light on the current imperialism of the supposedly borderless world of the electronic media and marketing machine of the transnational corporations?

JS Obviously it can.

JK What do you suggest be done to remedy historical misperceptions of the world outside of Europe and North America and why is it necessary to do this? Do we need a change in curricula? A relaxation of immigration restrictions concerning Muslims, concerning all?

JS I don't have a clear-cut blue print about how one ought to make the world a better place to live in. Obviously, however, all of what you mention is blatantly needed.

JK Yes, but I'd like to hear from you how you think curricula and the production of history could be changed, for example here in Québec where the working out of colonial dynamics can be observed firsthand.

JS I could rant on and on about the Québécois provincialist question — and the question of the teaching of history. Intellectuals at [Montréal's English Language daily] *The Gazette* think that students are being fed a revisionist view of things, with the oppression of the francophones in the foreground. Obviously — this is where it ties in with the themes of my trilogy — we need to teach wider and more complex historical contexts which are more inclusive of points-of-views thus far ignored. Banal-sounding, but there you have it.

113

JK Are you — with Kabbani and Huntington — concerned about an imminent clash of civilisations, and if so, in what form?

JS Wow! What do you mean? I just wanted to connect the past with the present.

APPENDIX A
SCREENINGS OF THE TRILOGY

The Raft of The Medusa:
five voices on colonies, nations and histories
Première, Cinéma Parallèle, Montréal, 21 Feb 1993
Canadian Film Studies Association, McGill University racism conference, Montréal, 18 Mar 1993
Desh Pardesh Festival, Toronto, 27 Mar 1993
Canadian Images, Toronto, Apr 1993
Prim Video: Fenêtre sur L'Orient, Montréal, Apr 1993
Canadian Film Studies Association, Ottawa, 2 Jun 1993
Saw Gallery, Ottawa, 3 Jun 1993
Festival da Gueira dal Oz, Portugal, 9-19 Sep 1993

Into the European Mirror
Première, Cinéma Parallèle, Montréal, 20 Feb 1994
One World festival, Ottawa, 19 Mar 1994
Dept. of Arabic Studies, The American University, Cairo, Jan 1994
"Imagining the Middle East: Screenings and Discussions on Politics and Representation," John Spotton Cinema, Toronto, 19 Jun 1994
Open Space, "Post-colonialism in the Commonwealth," Victoria, Jun 1994
Video Inn, Vancouver, Jun 1994

City of the Dead and the World Exhibitions
Première, Festival de nouveau cinèma et video, Montréal, Jun 1995
Cinéma Parallèle, Montréal, May 1995

APPENDIX B
AND THE CRITICS RAVED . . .

"This is the most polished of Julian Samuel's recent excursions into the colonial encounter. . . . There's a lot of expensive talk to take in, and as beautifully produced as some of the archival images are, they're used only to support the words. *Into the European Mirror* demands patience, but it offers the rewards of a good read."
NOW (Toronto), June 16, 1994.

"In his films, anger is subsumed into a fresh and provocative analysis of the postmodern world."
The Gazette (Montréal), June 11, 1995.

"Unfortunately, at the present moment, it is not possible for the Gallery to acquire this work [Raft] . . . . I would also suggest that you try to approach broadcasters with this videotape because I think it presents valuable ideas and raises interesting questions in a form suitable for the small screen."
National Gallery of Canada (Ottawa), May 26, 1993.

"Unfortunately, though the topic is interesting, we have decided against purchasing the program."
TV Ontario (Toronto), March 8, 1994.

"Although the Musée is without doubt interested in the various issues raised and addressed in your work, it considers the mainly documentary nature of it not to be concordant with the experimental artworks the institution has elected to collect."
Musée D'Art Contemporain de Montréal, November 29, 1993.

"... the persons interviewed were presented as figures of authority whom the viewer is not invited to question. Secondly, the didacticism of the presentation conflicted with the progressivism of the content. In the context of a progressive strain of twentieth century art. . . the best artists — Eisenstein, Brecht, Godard, Gilles Groulx, to name a few — have considered form and content inseparable one from the other, and have worked both together in their art."
National Gallery of Canada (Ottawa), July 23, 1993.

"Sorry, but I'm not interested in *Into the European Mirror.*"
BBC Documentaries (London), April 21, 1995.

". . . important theory delivered by articulate, thoughtful thinkers. But as I [sic] work committed to videotape, I found *The Raft* somewhat staid."
University of California at Berkeley, n.d.

"The work seems extremely engaging and provocative, and you are a most persuasive, articulate advocate. . . . I am sorry to write that we have no immediate screening context for the work. . ."
Walker Art Center (Minneapolis), January 5, 1995.

"For the time being I do see no real chance, we lost some time slots to the soccer-championships and suffer from program-overflow."
ORF Austrian Broadcasting Corp. (Vienna), April 21, 1995.

"The Prince of Wales was interested to read this but regrets that he is unable to reply personally. . . . I am sorry to have to send you such a disappointing reply. Nevertheless, His Royal Highness was grateful to you for writing and has asked me to send his best wishes."
St. James's Palace (London), June 30, 1995.

APPENDIX C
BIOGRAPHY OF JULIAN SAMUEL

Video producer, filmmaker, novelist and critic Julian Samuel was born in Lahore, Pakistan in 1952, five years after the Partition of India. In 1958, together with his family, he immigrated to the United Kingdom and attended school in Warlingham, Surrey. In 1966, the family again immigrated, this time to Downsview, Ontario, Canada.

In 1979, Samuel earned a BA in English literature at Trent University in Peterborough, Ontario. The same year he moved to Montréal to begin his MFA degree at Concordia University. He graduated in 1981 and later taught a film studies course at his Alma Mater. A self-described Pakistani-British-Canadian-Montréaler, Samuel considers "home" to be a conceptual device, "an idea that tries very conservatively to fix people."

In 1984-87, Samuel hosted a fifteen minute weekly radio show on events in the Third World broadcast on Radio Centreville.

His films and videos have been screened in New York at Millennium, (1980) and the Ten Years of Living Cinema (1982), Tyneside Film Festival (1982), the Havana Film Festival (1983), the London Filmmakers' Co-op (1987), the National Gallery of Canada (1989), the Festival da Gueira dal Oz in Portugal (1993), the American University in Cairo (1994), and Montréal's Le Nouveau Festival International Cinéma Vidéo (1995). His work is represented in several national collections and has been reviewed in many publications including: *Fuse, Matrix, Le Devoir, The Arab World Review, Cinema Canada, Ba.Zaar, McGill Daily* and *Now*. He has also published critical reviews and essays in many of the aforementioned journals. Samuel was Artist-in-residence at the Banff Centre in 1993 during which time he did the final edit of *Into the European Mirror.*

He has penned one collection of poetry, *Lone Ranger in Pakistan* (1986), and one novel, *Passage to Lahore* (1995), in addition to co-editing with Jocelyne Doray the book version of *Raft of the Medusa* (1993). His photographs and paintings have been shown in solo and group shows at independent galleries throughout Ontario.

introducing mimilon

APPENDIX D
FILMOGRAPHY, VIDEOGRAPHY & PUBLIC COLLECTIONS — JULIAN SAMUEL

City of the Dead and the World Exhibitions (1995) Hi8/Betacam SP, 76 min

Into the European Mirror (1994) Hi8/Betacam SP, 56 min

Raft of the Medusa: five voices on colonies, nations and histories (1993) Hi8/Betacam SP, 99 min

Red Star over the Western Press, Archive: Algeria; 1954-62 (1987) 3/4 inch, 84 min

Ministry of Revolution: the Concept of Terrorism in the Western Press (1985) 1/2 inch, 59 min

Interview with Two Africans (1985) 1/2 inch, 40 min

Free Nelson Mandela (1985) 1/2 inch, 8:30 min

Imperial Postcard (1984) 16mm, 6 min

Blood City Montréal (1984) 16mm, 6 min

Resisting the Pharaohs (1984) 16mm, 33:34 min

The Long Sleep and Big Goodbye (1983) 16mm, 14 min

Dictators (1982) 16mm, 6:30 min

In India and Pakistan (1981) 16mm, 50 min

Literature/Language/Film (1980) 16mm, 75 min

Black Skin White Masks (1980) 16mm, 5 min

Slight Sight: Sonata Towards Spring (1979) 16mm, 15 min

Portrait of I (1979) 16mm, 5 min

Portrait of C (1979) 16mm, 52 seconds

Formation (1976) 16mm, 11 min

National Gallery of Canada (Film - *Resisting the Pharaohs* and Video - *City of the Dead*)

Ontario Arts Council (stills)

National Film Board of Canada (stills)

National Television, Radio, and Sound Archives, Ottawa (films and videos)

McGill University (papers and the trilogy)

Concordia University (trilogy)

BIBLIOGRAPHY

Abley, Mark. "Film-maker is establishment's foe," *Montréal Gazette.* 11 June 1995:F3.

Abu-Lughod, Janet L. *Before European hegemony: the world system A.D. 1250-1350.* New York: Oxford University Press, 1989.

Achbar, Mark and Peter Wintonick. *Manufacturing consent: Noam Chomsky and the media.* Montréal: Necessary Illusions, National Film Board of Canada, 1992. (165 min.)

Ahmad, Aijaz. *In Theory: classes, nations, literatures.* London: Verso, 1992.

Ahmed, Akbar S. *Postmodernism and Islam: predicament and promise.* London, New York: Routledge, 1992.

Alioff, Maurie. "Points of Contact," (Review of *The Raft of the Medusa) Matrix.* Summer, 1993 40:83-4.

Baert, Renee. ed. *Territories of Difference.* Banff: The Walter Philips Gallery, 1993.

Bailey, Cameron. "Documentaries Highlight Desh Pardesh," *Now Magazine.* 18-24 March 1993.

———. "Julian Samuel takes tottering system to the edge," *Now Magazine.* 16-22 June 1994:50-1.

———. "Julian Samuel's Red Star over the Western Press," *Cinema Canada.* October 1987:39-40.

Baring, Evelyn, Lord Cromer. *Modern Egypt.* Vol. 2. New York: Macmillan, 1908.

Bhabha, Homi. *Nation and Narration.* London: Routledge, 1993.

Cavanagh, Chris. "Mangled media," (Review of "Resisting the Pharoahs") *McGill Daily.* 15 November 1984:4.

———. "Tonto's back and he's mad as hell," (Review of *Lone Ranger in Pakistan) McGill Daily Arts Supplement.* 15 January 1987:1-5.

Coulombe, Michel and Marcel Jean. *Le Dictionnaire du cinéma québécois.* Montréal: Boréal, 1988.

Cron, Marie-Michèle. "Un voile se lève sur l'Orient," *Le Devoir*. 28 April 1993.

Doray, Jocelyne and Julian Samuel, eds., *The Raft the of the Medusa: five voices on colonies, nations and histories*. Montréal: Black Rose Books, 1993.

Dowding, Martin. "Review: *Lone Ranger in Pakistan*," *What*. 1987 9:13-15.

Giannou, Chris. *Besieged: A Doctor's Story of Life and Death in Beirut*. Toronto: Key Porter Books, 1990.

Halbfass, Wilhelm. *India and Europe: an essay in philosophical understanding*. Delhi: Motilal Banarsidass, 1990.

Hentsch, Thierry. *Imagining the Middle East*. trans. Fred Reed. Montréal: Black Rose Books, 1992.

Huntington, Samuel. "The Coming Clash of Civilizations," *Foreign Affairs*. Summer 1993.

Kabbani, Rana. *Letter to Christendom*. London: Virago, 1989.

Maalouf, Amin. *Léon l'Africain*. Paris: J-C Lattès, 1986.

Majzels, Robert. "Drafting on the Medusa," *Harbour 8*. Fall 1993 2(4):39-41.

Mitchell, Timothy. *Colonising Egypt*. Cambridge: Cambridge University Press, 1988.

Nourbese Philip, Marlene. *Frontiers : selected essays and writings on racism and culture*. Stratford, Ont.: Mercury Press, 1992.

Piscatori, James P. *Islam in a World of Nation-States*. Cambridge: Cambridge University Press, 1986.

Posner, Michael. *Canadian Dreams: the making and marketing of independent films*. Vancouver: Douglas & McIntyre, 1993.

Said, Edward W. *Covering Islam: how the media and the experts determine how we see the rest of the world*. New York: Pantheon books, 1981.

———. *Orientalism*. New York: Vintage Books, 1978.

Salloum, Jayce, Walid Ra'ad. *Up to the South*. New York: Vidéographe (distributor), 1993. (60 min.)

———. *(This is Not Beirut) There was and there was not*. New York: Vidéographe (distributor), 1994. (48 min.)

Samuel, Julian. *Lone Ranger in Pakistan*. Peterborough: Emergency Press, 1986.

———. "Orientalism Reconsidered," *Europe and its Others*. 2 vols. Ed. Francis Baker et al. Colchester: University of Essex, 1985.

———. *Passage to Lahore*. Stratford: Mercury Press, 1995.

Sheridan, Chris. "Samuel looks through European Mirror," *McGill Daily*. 17 February 1994.

Siberok, Martin. "Another View: *The Raft of the Medusa* examines history from a non-European perspective," *Hour Magazine*, 22-28 April 1993.

———. "Fact Denial: Julian Samuel's *Into the European Mirror* examines Islam's contribution to European civilization," *Hour Magazine*, 17 February 1994.

Suleri, Sara. *The Rhetoric of English India*. Chicago: University of Chicago Press, 1992.

Tomlins, Colin. "A revolutionary effort in video," *Arab World Review*. June 1987: 11.

Young, Robert. *White Mythologies: Writing History and the West*. London: Routledge, 1990.

Also Published by

IMAGINING THE MIDDLE EAST
Thierry Hentsch

translated by Fred A. Reed

Recipient of the Governor General's Literary Award for Translation

For readers who want to understand the world of plural identities and the tactics of "appropriation," this is a very rich and necessary book.
Montréal Gazette
This Canadian professor adds to the critique of Orientalism... a stimulating work.
Journal of Palestine Studies
This remarkable book... could be seen as advancing our understanding beyond professor Edward Said's Orientalism.
Crescent
Fresh insights into the areas of the "mythical frontier"... a thorough and valuable account.
Arab Studies Quarterly

218 pages, index
Paperback ISBN: 1-895431-12-3 $19.99
Hardcover ISBN: 1-895431-13-1 $48.99

COMMON CENTS
Media Portrayal of the Gulf War and Other Events
James Winter

Objectivity is the theme of these five case studies which deal with how the media covered the Gulf War, the Oka standoff, the Ontario NDP's budget, the Meech Lake Accord and Free Trade. Winter shows how media coverage of events consistently casts them in what becomes a seemingly apolitical 'common-sense' framework, a framework which actually represents the opinions of the power elite.

Like Chomsky, he enjoys contrasting the "common-sense" interpretation with views from alternative sources. As facts and images clash, we end up with a better grasp of the issues at hand.
Montréal Gazette
Winter's analysis of why the media fail to tell us all, in greater, more useful depth, gives us some basis for hope and perhaps humor.
Peace Magazine

304 pages, index
Paperback ISBN: 1-895431-24-7 $23.99
Hardcover ISBN: 1-895431-25-5 $52.99

INDIGNANT HEART
A Black Worker's Journal
Charles Denby

A two-part account of a U.S. activist's battle for freedom, first personally and then as a supporter of the principal movements of the last twenty-five years.

295 pages
Paperback ISBN: 0-919618-67-7 $9.99
Hardcover ISBN: 0-919618-93-6 $38.99

BETWEEN THE LINES
How to Detect Bias and Propaganda in the News and Everyday Life
Eleanor MacLean

Taking professional journalism to task for not practising fully enough the lofty ideals it preaches.
Canadian Journal of Communication
An excellent resource tool for teachers.
Kingston Whig-Standard

296 pages
Paperback ISBN: 0-919619-12-6 $19.99
Hardcover ISBN: 0-919619-14-2 $48.99

BEYOND HYPOCRISY
Decoding the News in an Age of Propaganda
Including a Doublespeak Dictionary for the 1990s
Edward S. Herman

Illustrations by Matt Wuerker

In a highly original volume that includes an extended essay on the Orwellian use of language that characterizes U.S. political culture, cartoons, and a cross-referenced lexicon of *doublespeak* terms with examples of their all too frequent usage, Herman and Wuerker highlight the deception and hypocrisy contained in the U.S. government's favourite buzz-words.

Rich in irony and relentlessly forthright, Beyond Hypocrisy *is a valuable resource for those interested in avoiding... 'an unending series of victories over your own memory'.*
Montréal Mirror
Edward Herman starts out with a good idea and offers a hard-hitting and often telling critique of American public life.
Ottawa Citizen

239 pages, illustrations, index
Paperback ISBN: 1-895431-48-4 $19.99
Hardcover ISBN: 1-895431-49-2 $48.99

YEAR 501
The Conquest Continues
Noam Chomsky

2nd printing

A powerful and comprehensive discussion of the incredible injustices hidden in our history.

...Year 501 offers a savage critique of the new world order.
MacLean's Magazine
Tough, didactic, [Chomsky] skins back the lies of those who make decisions.
Globe and Mail
...a much-needed defense against the mind-numbing free market rhetoric.
Latin America Connexions

331 pages, index
Paperback ISBN: 1-895431-62-X $19.99
Hardcover ISBN: 1-895431-63-8 $48.99

JFK, the Vietnam War, and U.S. Political Culture
Noam Chomsky

For those who turn to Hollywood for history, and confuse creative license with fact, Chomsky proffers an arresting reminder that historical narrative rarely fits neatly into a feature film.

...a fascinating and disturbing portrait of the Kennedy dynasty.
Briarpatch
...the most important contribution to the ongoing public and private discussions about JFK.
Kitchener-Waterloo Record

172 pages, index
Paperback ISBN: 1-895431-72-7 $19.99
Hardcover ISBN: 1-895431-73-5 $48.99

ANARCHIST COLLECTIVES
Workers' Self-Management in Spain 1936-39
Sam Dolgoff, ed.

Introduction by Murray Bookchin

The eyewitness reports and commentary presented in this highly important study reveal a different understanding of the nature of socialism and the means for achieving it.
Noam Chomsky

195 pages, index, bibliography
Paperback ISBN: 0-919618-20-0 $16.99
Hardcover ISBN: 0-919618-21-9 $45.99

RACE, GENDER AND WORK
A Multi-Cultural Economic History of Women in the United States
Teresa Amott and Julie Matthaei

Race, Gender, and Work *is exciting because of its frank acknowledgement of difference among women. It is a volume that will inform and motivate scholars and activists.*
Julianne Malveaux, University of California, Berkeley
... a detailed, richly textured history of American working women.
Barbara Ehrenreich, author of The Worst Years of Our Lives

433 pages, index, appendices
Paperback ISBN: 0-921689-90-X $19.99
Hardcover ISBN: 0-921689-91-8 $48.99

BALANCE: ART AND NATURE
John Grande

Poses questions about our relationship to the natural world, our place in the stream of natural evolution and technological process, and the role of visual artists in understanding, and defining, society and nature.

Makes unexpected connections giving new insights into contemporary art.
Public Art Review
Grande's book contains a lot of ideas, all of which are thought-provoking.
 Globe and Mail
Grande's grasp of the details makes this book convincing.
Books In Canada
Offers interesting parallels between different aspects of public art.
Espace Sculptur

250 pages, photographs, index
Paperback ISBN: 1-551640-06-6 $19.99
Hardcover ISBN: 1-551640-07-4 $48.99

POLITICAL ECONOMY OF INTERNATIONAL LABOUR MIGRATION*
Hassan Gardezi

While former studies on labour migration have concentrated on its effect on GNP, foreign exchange earnings, and labour exporting countries' rates of investment, Gardezi's work refocuses attention on the migrant workers themselves, their hopes and aspirations, family and community life, and working conditions both at home and abroad. Taking this wide-ranging view, he is able to enhance our understanding of the transfers of labour force.

210 pages
Paperback ISBN: 1-551640-16-3 $19.99
Hardcover ISBN: 1-551640-17-1 $48.99

A PASSION FOR RADIO
Radio Waves and Community
Bruce Girard, ed.

A project of the World Association of Community Radio Broadcasters, this book tells the stories of alternative radio projects around the globe—stories about a passion for fundamental social change, in a great diversity of situations from First Nations in the Canadian North, to punks in Amsterdam, progressives in California, guerrillas in El Salvador, genuine revolutionaries in ex-Communist countries.

The stories in this book are moving and inspiring.
Media Development
This impressive book is an exciting window into the increasingly diffuse world of participatory media.
Media Information Australia

212 pages
Paperback ISBN: 1-895431-34-4 $19.99
Hardcover ISBN: 1-895431-35-2 $48.99

THE ECOLOGY OF FREEDOM
The Emergence and Dissolution of Hierarchy, revised edition
Murray Bookchin

The most systematic articulation of ideas.
San Francisco Review of Books
... a confirmation of his [Bookchin's] status as a penetrating critic not only of the ways in which humankind is destroying itself, but of the ethical imperative to live better.
The Village Voice
Elegantly written, and recommended for a wide audience.
Library Journal

395 pages, index,
Paperback ISBN: 0-921689-72-1 $19.99
Hardcover ISBN: 0-921689-73-X $48.99

RADICAL PRIORITIES: NOAM CHOMSKY
Carlos P. Otero, ed.

2nd revised edition, 4th printing

A fuller picture of Chomsky's fascinating political scholarship.
Harvard International Review
... another valuable collection of Chomsky's political and social criticism.
The Village Voice
We are indebted to the editor, C.P. Otero, for this collection.
The Humanist in Canada

307 pages
Paperback ISBN: 0-920057-17-9 $19.99
Hardcover ISBN: 0-920057-16-0 $48.99

MANUFACTURING CONSENT
Noam Chomsky And the Media
Mark Achbar, ed.

2nd printing

Manufacturing Consent Noam Chomsky and the Media, the companion book to the award-winning film, charts the life of America's most famous dissident, from his boyhood days running his uncle's newsstand in Manhattan to his current role as outspoken social critic.

A juicily subversive biographical/philosophical documentary bristling and buzzing with ideas.
Washington Post
You will see the whole sweep of the most challenging critic in modern political thought.
Boston Globe
One of our real geniuses... an excellent introduction.
Village Voice
An intellectually challenging crash course in the man's cooly contentious analysis, laying out his thoughts in a package that is clever and accessible.
Los Angeles Times
... challenging, controversial... the unravelling of ideas.
Globe and Mail
...lucid and coherent statement of Chomsky's thesis.
The Times of London
... invaluable as a record of a thinker's progress towards basic truth and basic decency.
The Guardian

264 pages, 270 illustrations, bibliography, index
Paperback ISBN: 1-551640-02-3 $19.99
Hardcover ISBN: 1-551640-03-1 $48.99

FRIENDLY FASCISM
The New Face of Power in America
Bertram Gross

A provocative and original study of current trends in the U.S. resulting in a forecast of totalitarianism.

Gross leaves the reader breathless. Friendly Fascism is historical and journalistic.
Fuse Magazine

410 pages, index
Paperback ISBN: 0-920057-23-3 $19.99
Hardcover ISBN: 0-920057-22-5 $48.99

DURRUTI
The People Armed
Abel Paz

translated by Nancy MacDonald

A history of the Spanish revolution, as well as being the story of Buenaventura Durruti, uncompromising anarchist, intransigent revolutionary,

Durruti talks new courage into men. When things go bad, he puts himself at the head. Wherever you go it's Durruti and Durruti again, spoken of as a wonder man.
Toronto Daily Star

323 pages, illustrated
Paperback ISBN: 0-919618-74-X $16.99
Hardcover ISBN: 0-919618-73-1 $45.99

CIVILIZATION AND ITS DISCONTENTED
John F. Laffey

Nominated for the 1993 QSPELL Award

This book, in three extended essays, investigates various beliefs about civilization. John Laffey explores its history and its common usage, and has devoted the final chapter to a look at the attitudes of Sigmund Freud.

The craft of the historian is to study the past and analyze it for present and future generations. Laffey certainly does this.

The academic community will recognize the merits of the work in its scholarship and research materials.
The Montréal Gazette

180 pages, index
Paperback ISBN: 1-895431-70-0 $16.99
Hardcover ISBN: 1-895431-71-9 $45.99

FEMINISM
Angela Miles and Geraldine Finn, eds.

2nd revised edition

A positive sign that feminism continues to be a healthy, growing movement that is joyfully redefining what it means to be fully human.
United Church Observer

...a very satisfying book... highly readable, well-argued, stimulating, and provocative... provides an alternative feminist framework to guide how scholarship and politics should be carried out.
Canadian Journal of Political Science

400 pages, bibliography
Paperback ISBN: 0-921689-22-5 $19.99
Hardcover ISBN: 0-921689-23-3 $48.99

HOT MONEY AND THE POLITICS OF DEBT
R.T. Naylor

2nd edition
Introduction by Leonard Silk, former financial editor of the New York Times

A ball of hot money rolls around the world. It seeks anonymity and political refuge: it dodges taxes and sidesteps currency controls; it rolls through shell companies and numbered accounts, phoney charities and religious foundations. And as the ball of hot money grows, so, too, does the international debt crisis. For hot money and the international debt are two sides of the same devalued coin.

As conspiracy theories go, here is one that is truly elegant. It involves everybody.
Washington Post
... a fascinating survey of international finance scams.
Globe and Mail
A startling and informative book which everyone... should read.
Lloyd's List
Naylor discusses the global pool of hot and homeless money... how it is used and abused.
Journal of Economic Literature

540 pages, index
Paperback ISBN: 1-895431-94-8 $19.99
Hardcover ISBN: 1-895431-95-6 $48.99
L.C. No. 94-071245

LOUISE MICHEL
Edith Thomas

translated by Penelope Williams

From the barricades of the Paris Commune to the spectacular trials and demonstrations, Louise Michel is one of the most extraordinary legends in the literature of freedom.

A very complete and very attractive biography, richly written.
Le Monde
Well done... especially the account of Louise's adaptation to life in New Caledonia.
American Historical Review

444 pages
Paperback ISBN: 0-919619-07-4 $19.99
Hardcover ISBN: 0-919619-08-2 $48.99

has also published the following books of related interest

The Raft of the Medusa: Five Voices on Colonies, Nations and Histories,
  by Jocelyn Doray and Julian Samuel
Imagining the Middle East, *by Thierry Hentsch*
Beyond O.J.: Race, Sex and Class Lessons for America,
  by Earl Ofari Hutchinson
Democracy's Oxygen: How the News Media Smother the Facts,
  by James Winter
Perspectives on Power: Reflections on Human Nature and the Social
  Order, *by Noam Chomsky*
Complicity: Human Rights and Canadian Foreign Policy, *by Sharon Scharfe*
From Camp David to the Gulf: Negotiations, Language and
  Propaganda, and War, *by Adel Safty*
World Inequality, *edited by Emmanuel Wallerstein*
Free Trade: Neither Free Nor About Trade, *by Christopher Merrett*
Mexico: Land and Liberty, Anarchist Influences in the Mexican
  Revolution, by Ricardo Flores Magon
The New World Order and the Third World, *edited by Dave Broad and
  Lori Foster*
Trilateralism: Elite Planning for World Management,
  edited by Holly Sklar
Balance: Art and Nature, *by John Grande*
Common Cents: Media Portaryal of the Gulf War and Other Events,
  by James Winter
Communication: For and Against Democracy, *by Marc Raboy
  and Peter A. Bruck, eds.*

send for a free catalogue of all our titles
BLACK ROSE BOOKS
C.P. 1258
Succ. Place du Parc
Montréal, Québec
H3W 2R3 Canada
To order books in North America: (phone) 1-800-565-9523 (fax) 1-800-221-9985
In Europe: (phone) 081-986-485 (fax) 081-533-5821

Our Web Site Address: http://www.web.net/blackrosebooks

*Printed by the workers of
Les Editions Marquis
Montmagny, Québec
for Black Rose Books Ltd.*